I0824496

Femke Vindevogel is a Flemish crochet designer who inherited the love of crochet from her grandmother and mother. As a child, Femke designed clothes for her dolls and her love for designing has only increased since then.

She is a product developer for Katia Yarns and Scheepjes yarn and her designs have featured in *Better Homes & Gardens* and *The Sewing Box* magazines. Femke is also an artist and a writer and has published several literary novels.

Femke has a big social media presence, with 30k followers on Instagram.

Instagram: @sweetamigurumidesign

Her first craft book, *Peter Panda and Pals*, has now sold in excess of 20k copies.

Also by Femke

978-1-80092-154-2

Kate Koala and Pals

First published in 2026
Search Press Limited
Wellwood, North Farm Road,
Tunbridge Wells, Kent TN2 3DR

1 2 3 4 5 6 7 8 9 10

ISBN: 978-1-80092-334-8
eBook ISBN: 978-1-80093-321-7

Bookmarked Hub

Extra copies of the templates are also available to download free from the Bookmarked Hub. Search for this book by title or ISBN: the files can be found under 'Book Extras'. Membership of the Bookmarked online community is free: www.bookmarkedhub.com

Publishers' notes

Metric measurements are used in this book; the imperial conversions are rounded to the nearest 1⁄16in. Always use either metric or imperial measurements, not a combination of both.

UK crochet terms are used throughout this book. For UK to US conversions, please refer to page 10.

The Publishers and author can accept no responsibility for any consequences arising from the information, advice or instructions given in this publication.

For errata, please visit our website (www.searchpress.com) or the Bookmarked Hub (www.bookmarkedhub.com).

About the author

You are invited to visit the author's Instagram: @sweetamigurumidesign

GPSR information can be found at www.searchpress.com
Printed in China, TT122025

Safety notice

Please be advised that safety eyes can be a choking hazard for young children, so avoid giving toys containing safety eyes to young children while unsupervised.

Kate Koala and Pals

10 SWEET AND EASY AMIGURUMI DESIGNS TO CROCHET

Femke Vindevogel

Contents

Dedication

Many thanks to my friend Caroline for all the first class advice and logistical help.

Acknowledgements

Thank you to Scheepjes for supplying me with yarn.

Introduction

I'm very pleased to present my second crochet book. From Puck Pugsie who travels nowhere without his memory foam pillow to Theodore Teddy who braids glow-in-the-dark friendship bracelets for everyone who is scared of the dark, I hope you will love these new characters as much as I have enjoyed designing them.

I have used organic yarn as much as possible, partly because it is soft and matt and pleasant to crochet with, but also because I care about the environment and want to be sustainable whenever I can.

My first book *Peter Panda and Pals* has been translated into four languages and it is still travelling around the globe.

I'm very grateful for that, and since then I've designed patterns for several yarn companies, given interviews, organized my first workshops and have been published in yarn magazines. It has been a rollercoaster!

Crochet designing is such a pleasure to me, and a nice pink counterweight for the heavy themes in the literary novels and poetry I write. It's such a joyous thing to do, especially on rainy or cloudy days. And I'm Flemish, so we have lots of those days here!

I wish you lots of rainy crochet days too,

Femke

@sweetamigurumidesign

Tools and materials

Yarn and crochet hooks

My favourite brands have a soft, matt finish. I use 4-ply (fingering) yarn and a 2mm (UK 14, US 0) crochet hook for most of the toys. Some of the larger toys are crocheted with 5-ply (sport) yarn and a larger hook. I have indicated within each pattern which yarn and hook I have used. You can replace all these yarns with yarns in the same weight category. If you use bigger yarn, your doll will be bigger.

For amigurumi, always use a smaller hook than recommended for the yarn that you are using. I usually go down a full size. This gives a neater finish and a nice result. If you use a bigger hook than indicated, your toy will be less tight and the stuffing will show. My favourite hooks are Tulip hooks: I love the ergonomic feel of them and they last a long time.

Safety eyes

These are plastic eyes with a backing washer that stops the eye coming off your toy. They are easy to attach but difficult to remove, making them ideal to use on toys for older children. However, when you crochet toys for children under three years old, you should embroider the eyes instead.

Basic kit

You will also need the following:

Embroidery thread Use dark brown and black thread to embroider eyes, snouts and small details. My favourite brand is DMC.

Scissors Use small, sharp scissors for cutting ends.

Soft synthetic stuffing I love using polyester fibrefill for stuffing. It is cheap, washable and hypoallergenic.

Stitch markers When you crochet in spirals, place a stitch marker at the beginning of each round to help count your stitches.

Pins Use round-headed pins to mark the position of body parts before embroidering them. Also, use pins to mark the centre of the face, so you know where to embroider facial details.

Tapestry needle (not pictured) I use this for assembling the large pieces of the toys. I love the bent-tip needle by Clover.

Embroidery needle (not pictured) Use a small, sharp needle for sewing smaller parts and embroidery.

Textile glue (not pictured) Some parts of the toys are glued rather then sewn. I use a transparent textile glue such as HT2 from Gütermann Creativ.

Pompom maker (not pictured) This is useful for adding pompoms to hats or scarves.

Scheepjes
STONE WASHED
Scheepjes
STONE WASHED
Catona
Lot:1131
6/0 3.50MM
5/0 3.00MM

Pattern notes

Abbreviations

bl	back loop
ch	chain
dc	double crochet
dc2tog	double crochet 2 together
dtr	double treble crochet
htr	half treble crochet
sl st	slip stitch
st	stitch
tr	treble crochet

UK/US terms

All the patterns are written using UK crochet terms. The equivalent US terms are below:

UK	US
double crochet	single crochet
double treble crochet	treble crochet
half treble crochet	half double crochet
treble crochet	double crochet

Key for difficulty

The patterns are for different abilities, so each pattern is marked with a skill level:

Beginner

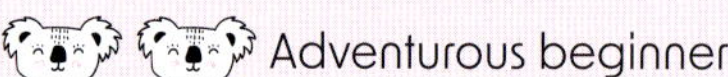

Adventurous beginner

Intermediate

If you have little experience crocheting amigurumi, I suggest starting with a beginner pattern. Once you have completed that and are feeling a bit more adventurous, work up to the adventurous beginner and intermediate patterns.

Basic kit

Where I refer to 'Basic kit' in the 'You will need' section of the patterns, please refer back to page 8.

Crochet techniques

Adjustable ring

Also known as a magic ring:

1 Create a loop by crossing the working end of the yarn (the yarn nearest the ball), then go through the loop with your hook and 'catch' the yarn.

2 Pull the yarn through the loop.

3 You'll now have a loop on your hook, and the ring which you'll work into. To secure the ring, wrap the working end around your hook and pull this through the loop to make a slip stitch.

4 Start to make dc stitches into the ring. To do this, insert your hook into the ring and pull the working yarn through it; you now have two loops on your hook. Yarn over hook, and pull through both loops on your hook. You'll now have 1 dc worked into the ring! Most patterns in this book start with 6 dc worked into the ring.

5 Pull the tail end of the yarn to close the ring and make a small circle without a hole. You now have an adjustable ring.

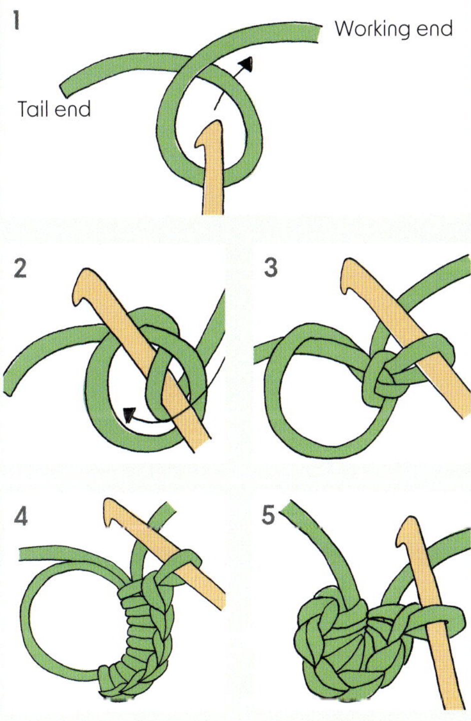

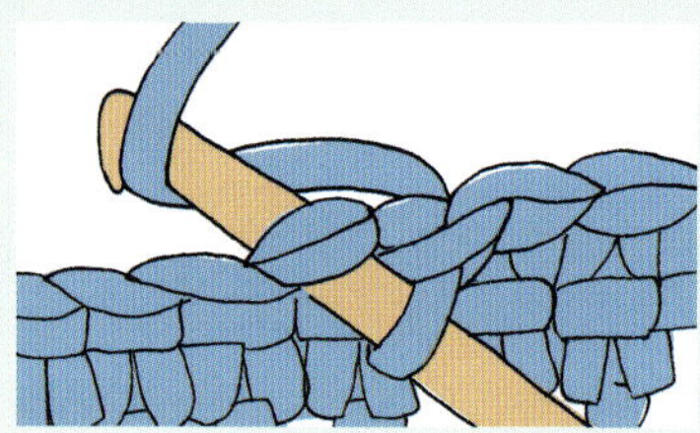

X-shaped double crochet with yarn under.

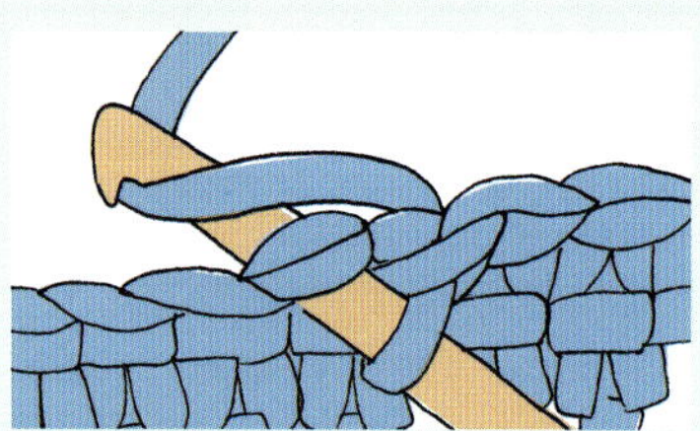

V-shaped double crochet with yarn over.

X-shaped double crochet (dc)

If not otherwise indicated, the dolls in this book are crocheted with an x-shaped double crochet stitch. This crochet stitch is tight, small and gives a neat result.

To get an x-shaped stitch you wrap your yarn *under* your hook, instead of wrapping it over:

1 Insert the hook into the stitch and yarn under.

2 Pull the yarn through the first loop. Yarn over. Pull the yarn through the two remaining loops on the hook.

If you are not familiar with this stitch, you can use a v-shaped double crochet instead.

Sewing open pieces together

For many of the toys, you will need to join open pieces together, using whip stitch.

1 Keep the two pieces against each other with the top of the stitches aligned. Insert the needle, going under both loops, from front to back.

2 Go through the next stitch of the first piece, inserting the needle under both loops, going back to front. Draw the stitch tight.

Invisible decrease

For best results, I always use an invisible decrease, but a normal decrease also works fine.

1 Insert the hook in the front loop of the first stitch.
2 Insert the hook in the front loop of the next stitch. You have three loops on the hook.
3 Yarn over and draw the yarn through the first two loops on the hook.
4 Yarn over again (4a) and draw the yarn through the two loops remaining on the hook (4b).

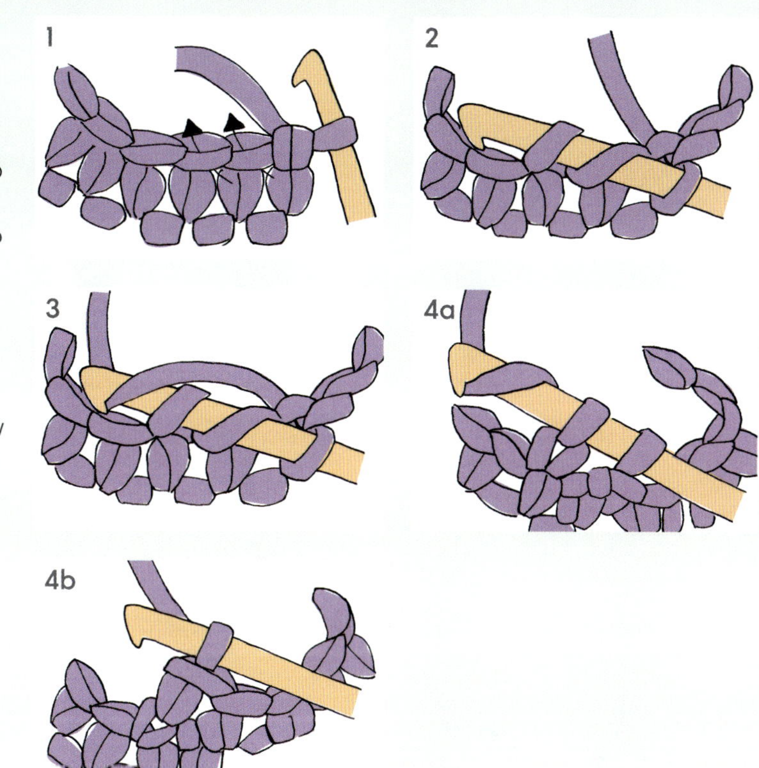

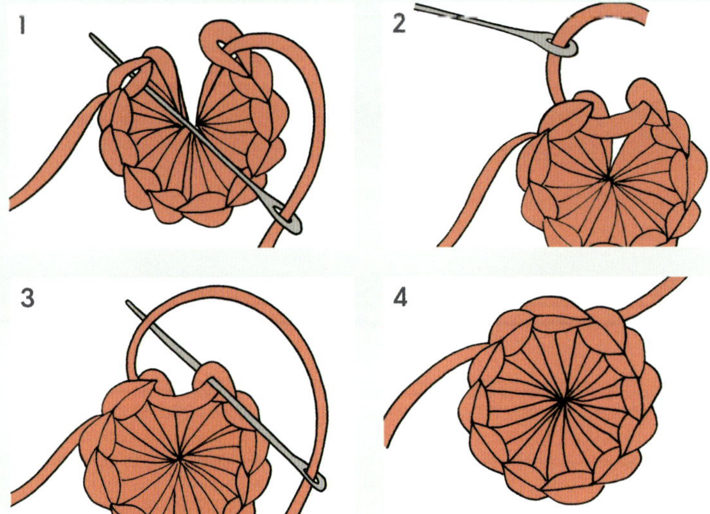

Invisible finish

Cut the yarn, leaving an end. Pull the hook up all the way to unravel the loop on your hook. Remember not to yarn over first like in the traditional method. Then thread the yarn end on the yarn/ tapestry needle.

1 Skip a stitch and insert the needle underneath the top (both loops – front and back) of the double crochet.
2 Pull the yarn loosely through to the back and you've created a front loop.
3 Go back and insert the needle underneath the back loop only of the last double crochet made in this round.
4 This will create the back loop.

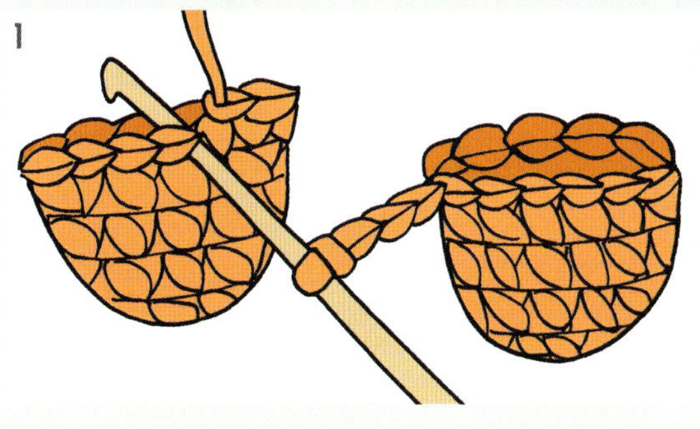

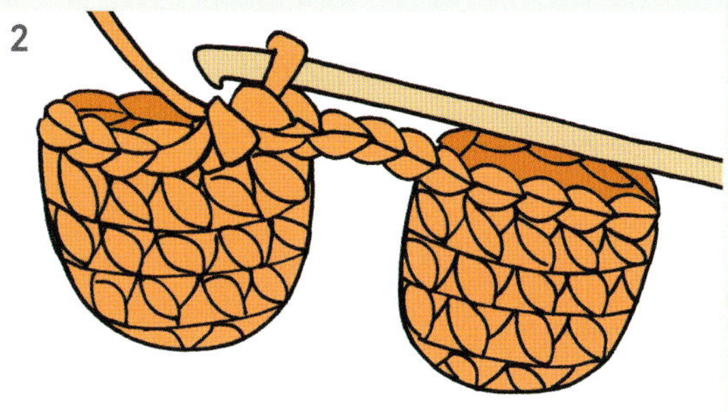

Joining legs together

For many of the toys, you will need to join the legs together.

1 Finish the first paw and fasten off. Finish the second paw and join, but do not fasten off and join the legs with a chain. The dc stitches will be worked into the loop of the chains.

2 Insert the hook into the stitch after the last stitch (the second to last round). This new stitch is the first stitch of the next round.

Changing colour

Always change colour by joining the new colour during the final step of the last stitch in the old colour.

Join in a new colour on the last yarn over, then pull it through the last two loops for double crochet, treble crochet and double treble crochet; for half treble crochet, pull it through the last three loops on the hook.

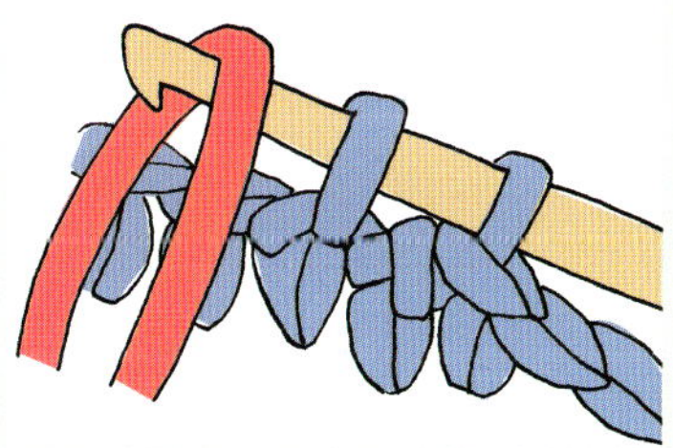

Short rows

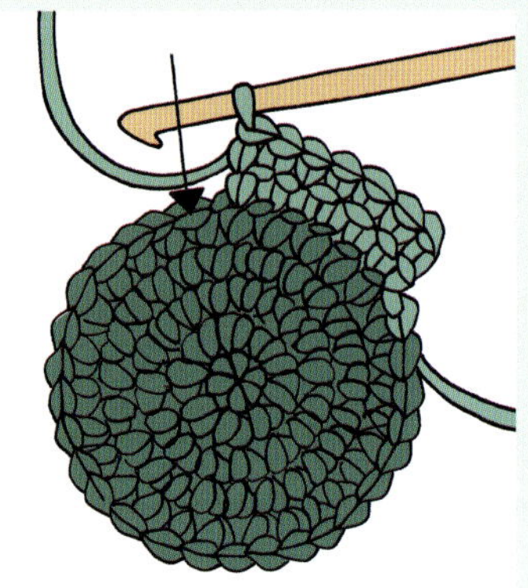

This technique involves crocheting incomplete rows or rounds, leaving stitches untouched, then turning your work before reaching the end. To avoid bulk, you don't make a turning chain while turning your work, you just crochet in the first stitch of the hook, instead of the second.

1 Crochet the indicated amount of dc stitches.
2 Turn your work to the wrong side of the work, *without* a turning chain, crochet the indicated amount of stitches, start in the first stitch from the hook, instead of the second and leave the last stitch unworked.
3 Turn your work to the right side *without* a turning chain, and again crochet the indicated amount of stitches. Start crocheting in the first stitch from the hook.
4 Crochet on in stitch with black arrow (see illustration), pull the yarn tight to prevent a gap.
5 Once you've crocheted around, you'll reach the beginning of the short row. Crochet in the first stitch of the short rows, there is a large height difference. When closing the short row, pull the yarn tight to prevent a gap.

Joining a new colour in a granny flower

1 Make a slip knot.
2 Insert your hook into an indicated space or stitch. Pull the yarn through, so that the knot is on the back of the work. Tighten the slip knot.
3 Yarn over and pull the yarn through the loop.

Kate Koala

Kate is the coolest girl in the neighbourhood.
Every day, rain or shine, she fearlessly surfs the ocean.
When the sun sets, she chills with her friends around the campfire, drinking virgin mojitos and playing the didgeridoo.

You will need

– Basic kit (see page 8)

– 2mm (UK 14, US 0) crochet hook

– 2.5mm (UK 12/13, US 1/2) crochet hook

– Yarn:

• 6 balls of 4-ply (fingering), 100% cotton, 50g/1¾oz/170m/186yd. I used Annell Cotton 8 in light grey 57 (A), white 43 (B), soft pink 33 (C), dark pink 77 (D), dark grey 58 (E) and Scheepjes Organicon in bright ocean 215 (F)

– 2 dark brown safety eyes, 7mm (¼in)

– Dark grey felt

– Small piece of firm cardboard

I am 15cm (6in) tall

Legs and lower body

Start with the first leg.

Round 1: using yarn A and a 2mm (UK 14, US 0) hook, 8 dc in an adjustable ring (8 sts).

Close the ring with a sl st, ch 1.

Round 2: 1 dc in the back loop of each st (8 sts).

Round 3: *3 dc, 2 dc in next st*, twice (10 sts).

Round 4: *4 dc, 2 dc in next st*, twice (12 sts).

Round 5: *5 dc, 2 dc in next st*, twice (14 sts).

Round 6: change to yarn B, 1 dc in each st (14 sts).

Fasten off. Crochet the second leg, but do not fasten off.

Round 7: join the two legs as follows: ch 4 at the end of the second leg, 14 dc (one in every stitch of the first leg), ch 4, 14 dc in the second leg (4 + 14 + 4 + 14 = 36 sts). See page 15 for technique.

Round 8: 1 dc in each st (36 sts).

Round 9: *8 dc, 2 dc in next st*, three times, 9 dc (39 sts).

Round 10: 10 dc, 2 dc in next st, 9 dc, 2 dc in next st, 8 dc, 2 dc in next st, 9 dc (42 sts).

Round 11: 11 dc, 2 dc in next st, *9 dc, 2 dc in next st*, twice, 10 dc (45 sts).

Round 12: 11 dc, 2 dc in next st, *10 dc, 2 dc in next st*, twice, 11 dc (48 sts).

Rounds 13–23: 1 dc in each st (48 sts).

Round 24: 14 dc, dc2tog, 5 dc, dc2tog, 6 dc, dc2tog, 6 dc, dc2tog, 9 dc (44 sts).

Round 25: 1 dc in each st (44 sts).

Stitch up the hole between the two legs and start stuffing the legs and lower body.

Round 26: 13 dc, dc2tog, 20 dc, dc2tog, 7 dc (42 sts).

Round 27: 1 dc in each st (42 sts).

Round 28: *5 dc, dc2tog*, six times (36 sts).

Round 29: *4 dc, dc2tog*, six times (30 sts).

Round 30: 1 dc in each st (30 sts).

Fasten off.

Stuff the legs and body firmly.

Head

Round 1: using yarn A and a 2mm (UK 14, US 0) hook, 6 dc in an adjustable ring (6 sts).
Round 2: 2 dc in each st (12 sts).
Round 3: *1 dc, 2 dc in next st*, six times (18 sts).
Round 4: *2 dc, 2 dc in next st*, six times (24 sts).
Round 5: *3 dc, 2 dc in next st*, six times (30 sts).
Round 6: *4 dc, 2 dc in next st*, six times (36 sts).
Round 7: *5 dc, 2 dc in next st*, six times (42 sts).
Round 8: *6 dc, 2 dc in next st*, six times (48 sts).
Rounds 9–19: 1 dc in each st (48 sts).
Round 20: *6 dc, dc2tog*, six times (42 sts).
Round 21: 1 dc in each st (42 sts).
Round 22: *5 dc, dc2tog*, six times (36 sts).
Round 23: *4 dc, dc2tog*, six times (30 sts).
Fasten off, leaving an end for sewing. Stuff the head firmly.

Attach the safety eyes between rounds 14 and 15 with 10 stitches in between. Using the dark grey felt and the template below, cut out the nose. Glue the felt centred between the eyes, over rounds 14–18. Using yarn C, embroider the cheeks next to the eyes (see picture for position). Sew the head onto the body.

Nose template

For placement of nose, see picture.

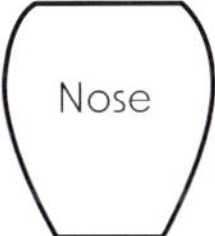

Arms (make 2)

Round 1: using yarn A and a 2mm (UK 14, US 0) hook, 5 dc in an adjustable ring (5 sts).
Round 2: 2 dc in each st (10 sts).
Rounds 3–10: 1 dc in each st (10 sts).
Rounds 11–13: change to yarn B, 1 dc in each st (10 sts).
Fasten off, leaving an end for sewing.
Gently stuff the front of the arms. Sew the arms onto the body on either side at round 29.

Tail

Round 1: using yarn B and a 2mm hook (UK 14, US 0), 6 dc in an adjustable ring (6 sts).
Round 2: 2 dc in each st (12 sts).
Round 3: *dc2tog*, six times (6 sts).
Fasten off, leaving an end for sewing the tail onto the body. Gently stuff the tail. Weave your yarn through the front loop of each st and pull. Sew the tail to the body centred between the legs across rounds 11–14.

Ears (make 2)

Step 1: inner part of the ear (make 4).
Round 1: using yarn B and a 2mm (UK 14, US 0) hook, 6 dc in an adjustable ring (6 sts).
Round 2: 2 dc in each st (12 sts).
Round 3: *1 dc, 2 dc in next st*, six times (18 sts).
Round 4: *2 dc, 2 dc in next st*, six times (24 sts).
Fasten off, end with an invisible finish.

Step 2: using yarn A, take 2 inner parts, place the wrong sides together, and crochet the parts together with v-shaped dc stitches. Crochet a dc in each st, through both loops (4 loops) and through both inner parts (24 sts).

Step 3: sl st in each st (24 sts). Fasten off, leaving an end for sewing the ear onto the head. Flatten the ears and sew onto the head (rounds 9–13, 22 sts in between). The ears are not stuffed.

Scarf

The scarf is crocheted with a bigger hook to make it fall more loosely.
Round 1: using yarn D and a 2.5mm (UK 12/13, US 1/2) hook, ch 39 (39 sts).
Round 2: join into the ring with a sl st, ch 1, 38 htr (39 sts).
Round 3: change to yarn B, 1 htr in each st (39 sts).
Round 4: change to yarn F, 1 htr in each st (39 sts).
Round 5: change to yarn B, 1 htr in each st (39 sts).
Round 6: change to yarn D, 1 htr in each st (39 sts).
Fasten off with an invisible finish. Weave in the ends. Pull the scarf up over the legs.

Surfboard

White section

Round 1: using yarn B and a 2mm (UK 14, US 0) hook, 9 dc in an adjustable ring (9 sts).
Round 2: 2 dc in each st (18 sts).
Round 3: 1 dc in each st (18 sts).
Round 4: *2 dc, 2 dc in next st*, six times (24 sts).
Round 5: 1 dc in each st (24 sts).
Round 6: 2 dc in first st, 11 dc, 2 dc in next st, 11 st (26 sts).

Rounds 7–19: 1 dc in each st (26 sts).
Fasten off with an invisible finish. Weave in the end.

Turquoise section

Round 1: using yarn F and a 2mm (UK 14, US 0) hook, 4 dc in an adjustable ring (4 sts).
Round 2: 2 dc in each st (8 sts).
Round 3: *3 dc, 2 dc in next st*, twice (10 sts).
Round 4: *4 dc, 2 dc in next st*, twice (12 sts).
Round 5: 1 dc in each st (12 sts).
Round 6: *3 dc, 2 dc in next st*, three times (15 sts).
Round 7: 1 dc in each st (15 sts).
Round 8: *4 dc, 2 dc in next st*, three times (18 sts).
Round 9: 1 dc in each st (18 sts).
Round 10: *8 dc, 2 dc in next st*, twice (20 sts).
Rounds 11 and 12: 1 dc in each st (20 sts).
Round 13: *9 dc, 2 dc in next st*, twice (22 sts).
Round 14: 1 dc in each st (22 sts).
Round 15: *10 dc, 2 dc in next st*, twice (24 sts).
Round 16: 1 dc in each st (24 sts).
Round 17: *11 dc, 2 dc in next st*, twice (26 sts).
Rounds 18–34: 1 dc in each st (26 sts).
Fasten off with an invisible finish, leaving an end for sewing. Do not stuff the board. Flatten the parts with a steam iron. Do not iron directly on your work but place a kitchen towel in between.

Back fin

Round 1: using yarn B and a 2mm (UK 14, US 0) hook, 4 dc in an adjustable ring (4 sts).
Round 2: *1 dc, 2 dc in next st*, twice (6 sts).
Round 3: *1 dc, 2 dc in next st*, three times (9 sts).
Round 4: *2 dc, 2 dc in next st*, three times (12 sts).
Round 5: 1 dc in each st (12 sts).
Round 6: *3 dc, 2 dc in next st*, three times (15 sts).
Round 7: 5 dc, 5 htr, 5 dc (15 sts).
Fasten off, leaving an end for sewing.
Do not stuff. Flatten and sew vertically onto the back of the board over rounds 3–10, see picture for position.

Leash

Using yarn E and a 2mm (UK 14, US 0) hook, ch 20. Close the ring with a sl st, ch 40. Fasten off, leaving an end for sewing the leash to the surfboard. Use an end to tighten up the sl st and weave it in. With the other end, sew the leash on the white part at front of the surfboard in the centre of round 3.

Sew the back fin on the board. Cut out a piece of firm cardboard that has the shape of the board. Slide the parts of the board over the cardboard. Sew the two parts of the board together.

Magnus Moose

Magnus likes long forest walks and knitting. Once a week he exchanges the woods for the city to attend a knitting group where he, alongside Stevie Snail and other friends, primarily eats Scottish shortbread and knits Nordic sweaters.

You will need

– Basic kit (see page 8)

– 2.5mm (UK 12/13, US 1/2) crochet hook

– Yarn:

• 3 balls of 5-ply (sport), 78% cotton, 22% acrylic, 50g/1¾oz/130m/142yd. I used Scheepjes Stone Washed in brown agate 822 (A), pink quartzite 821 (B) and black onyx 803 (C)

• 3 balls of 4-ply (fingering), 100% mercerized cotton, 50g/1¾oz/125m/137yd. I used Scheepjes Catona in fir 525 (D), rose wine 396 (E) and silver blue 528 (F)

– 2 safety eyes, 8mm (5⁄16in)

– Stitch markers

– Pompom maker

I am 28cm (11in) tall including my hat

Neck and body

Start by crocheting the neck.

Round 1: using yarn A and a 2.5mm (UK 12/13, US 1/2) hook, ch 24. Join the foundation chain with a sl st. Continue working in a spiral (24 sts).

Rounds 2 and 3: 1 dc in each st (24 sts).

Rounds 4 and 5: change to yarn B, 1 dc in each st (24 sts).

Round 6: ch 15. Place a stitch marker in the next st (this will be the beginning of each round from now). Crochet back on the chain: 2 dc in the second chain from the hook, 1 dc in the next 13 ch, 1 dc in the st where the foundation chain starts, continue on the neck, 1 dc in the next 24 dc, continue on the other side of the chain, 1 dc in the next 13 ch, 2 dc in the last ch (55 sts).

Round 7: 2 dc in the first st, 2 dc in next st, 52 dc, 2 dc in next st (58 sts).

Round 8: *1 dc, 2 dc in next st*, twice, 52 dc, 2 dc in next st, 1 dc (61 sts).

Round 9: 1 dc, 2 dc in next st, 2 dc, 2 dc in next st, 54 dc, 2 dc in next st, 1 dc (64 sts).

Round 10: *2 dc in first st, 2 dc*, twice, 2 dc in next st, 54 dc, 2 dc in next st, 2 dc (68 sts).

Rounds 11–21: 1 dc in each st (68 sts).

Legs

It's really helpful to divide the work and place some colourful stitch markers before you start on the legs.

The legs are (on the side) 8 sts apart and on the back and front 4 sts apart. (I've used red markers for the middle back and middle front stitch, blue and yellow for the front legs and green and pink for the back legs, see picture).

First find the middle back stitch of the moose's body. If you are not already there, crochet until the back middle stitch. Then, work 2 dc. Place a stitch marker in the next st and work 11 dc. (The first stitch of these 11 sts is the one with the stitch marker.) Ch 7. Join the last chain and the st with the stitch marker with a sl st.

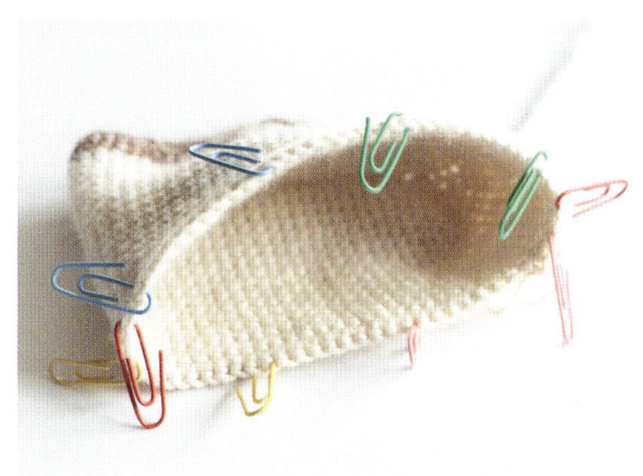

Back leg 1

The first leg will be formed with 11 sts of the body and 7 sts from the foundation chain.

Round 1: 18 dc (11 sts on the body and 7 on the chain) (18 sts).
Rounds 2–4: 1 dc in each st (18 sts).
Round 5: using yarn D, 1 dc in each st (18 sts).
Rounds 6 and 7: using yarn B, 1 dc in each st (18 sts).
Rounds 8 and 9: using yarn D, 1 dc in each st (18 sts).
Rounds 10 and 11: using yarn A, 1 dc in each st (18 sts).
Round 12: 16 dc, dc2tog (17 sts).
Round 13: 1 dc in each st (17 sts).
Round 14: 15 dc, dc2tog (16 sts).
Round 15: 1 dc in each st (16 sts).
Round 16: 14 dc, dc2tog (15 sts).
Round 17: 1 dc in each st (15 sts).
Round 18: *1 dc, dc2tog*, five times (10 sts).
Round 19: *dc2tog*, five times (5 sts).
Fasten off, leaving an end. Weave the yarn through the front loop of each remaining st and pull tight.

Front leg 1

Count 8 sts from the first back leg and attach yarn B to the ninth st, 11 dc, ch 7, join the last ch and the first st with a sl st.
Rounds 1–19: repeat rounds 1–19 of the back leg.

Front leg 2

Count 4 sts from the first front leg and attach yarn B in the fifth st, 11 dc, ch 7 and join the last ch and the first st with a sl st.
Rounds 1–19: repeat rounds 1–19 of the other legs.

Attaching front leg 1.

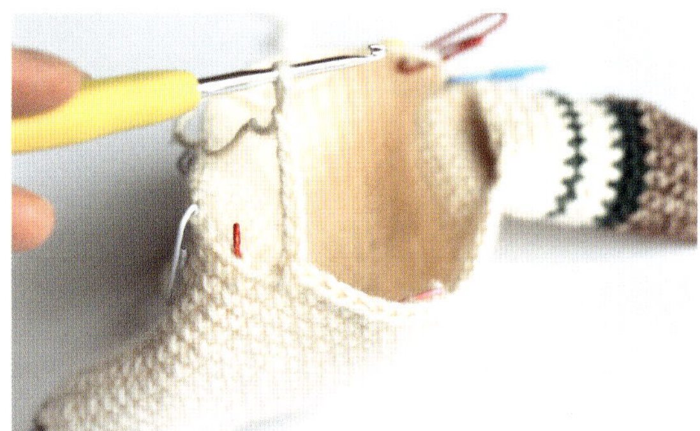

Back leg 2

Count 8 sts from the first front leg and attach yarn B in the ninth st, 11 dc, ch 7, join the last ch and the first st with a sl st.
Rounds 1–19: repeat rounds 1–19 of the other legs.

Embroidery on the body

First, embroider the green cross stitch between rounds 6 and 7 on each leg (leave a stitch between each cross stitch). Then, embroider some bigger snowflake stitches on the body (cross stitch with an extra horizontal line).

Tummy

Crochet a flap that will form the tummy.
Using yarn B, start with the 8-st space along the side. Attach yarn B to the first st next to the first leg. Crochet in rows.
Rows 1–14: 8 dc, 1 ch to turn (8 sts).
Fasten off, leaving an end for sewing.

Flap between legs (make 2)

Crochet a flap in the 4-st space between the front legs. Crochet in rows.
Rows 1–4: using yarn B, 4 dc, 1 ch to turn (4 sts).
Fasten off, leaving an end for sewing. Make another flap in the 4-st space between the back legs.

The tummy flap and flap between legs.

Closing the tummy flap.

Assembling the lower body

Sew the back flap to both back legs and the front flap to both front legs. Stuff the legs very firmly, especially the back legs and back body.
Sew the tummy flap to the other side of the moose. Then sew the tummy flap to all four legs and the flaps between them. Stuff very firmly as you go.

Sweater collar

The collar is crocheted in rows.

Row 1: using yarn D and a 2.5mm (UK 12/13, US 1/2) hook, ch 8, plus 1 ch to turn (8 sts).

Row 2: starting in the second ch from the hook, work 8 dc, 1 ch to turn (8 sts).

Row 3: 8 dc in bl, 1 ch to turn (8 sts).

Repeat row 3 until the collar fits around the neck. Fold in half lengthwise. Sew collar together along the bottom (lengthwise after folding). Sew the ends together (while around the neck).

Tail

Using yarn A and a 2.5mm (UK 12/13, US 1/2) hook, ch 5 (5 sts).

Starting in the second ch from the hook, 4 sl st (4 sts).

Fasten off, leaving an end for sewing. Sew the tail onto the back of the body on round 13.

Head

Round 1: using yarn A and a 2.5mm (UK 12/13, US 1/2) hook, 6 dc in an adjustable ring (6 sts).
Round 2: 2 dc in each st (12 sts).
Round 3: *1 dc, 2 dc in next st*, six times (18 sts).
Round 4: *2 dc, 2 dc in next st*, six times (24 sts).
Round 5: *3 dc, 2 dc in next st*, six times (30 sts).
Round 6: *4 dc, 2 dc in next st*, six times (36 sts).
Round 7: *5 dc, 2 dc in next st*, six times (42 sts).
Rounds 8–16: 1 dc in each st (42 sts).
Round 17: *5 dc, dc2tog*, six times (36 sts).
Rounds 18–24: 1 dc in each st (36 sts).
Stuff the head firmly as you go.
Round 25: *5 dc, 2 dc in next st*, six times (42 sts).
Round 26: 1 dc in each st (42 sts).
Round 27: *6 dc, 2 dc in next st*, six times (48 sts).
Rounds 28–37: 1 dc in each st (48 sts).
Round 38: *6 dc, dc2tog*, six times (42 sts).
Round 39: *5 dc, dc2tog*, six times (36 sts).
Attach the safety eyes between rounds 24 and 25, with 9 sts in between.
Round 40: *4 dc, dc2tog*, six times (30 sts).
Round 41: *3 dc, dc2tog*, six times (24 sts).
Round 42: *2 dc, dc2tog*, six times (18 sts).
Round 43: *1 dc, dc2tog*, six times (12 sts).
Round 44: *dc2tog*, six times (6 sts).
Fasten off, leaving a tail. Weave the yarn through the front loop of each remaining stitch and pull tight. Weave in the ends.

Cheeks (make 2)

Round 1: using yarn E and a 2.5mm (UK 12/13, US 1/2) hook, 8 dc in an adjustable ring (8 sts).
Fasten off with an invisible finish, leaving a tail for sewing and weave in the ends.
Glue or sew the cheeks onto the head, diagonally below the eyes (see picture for position).

Nostrils (make 2)

Round 1: using yarn C and a 2.5mm (UK 12/13, US 1/2) hook, 3 dc in an adjustable ring (3 sts).
Round 2: 2 dc in each st (6 sts).
Fasten off with an invisible finish, leaving an end for sewing, and weave in the ends.
Sew the nostrils onto the muzzle (see picture for position).

Ears (make 2)

Round 1: using yarn A and a 2.5mm (UK 12/13, US 1/2) hook, 5 dc in an adjustable ring (5 sts).
Round 2: 1 dc in each st (5 sts).
Round 3: 2 dc in each st (10 sts).
Round 4: 1 dc in each st (10 sts).
Round 5: *1 dc, 2 dc in next st*, five times (15 sts).
Round 6: 1 dc in each st (15 sts).
Round 7: *2 dc, 2 dc in next st*, five times (20 sts).
Rounds 8 and 9: 1 dc in each st (20 sts).
Fasten off, leaving an end for sewing.
Do not stuff the ears.
Flatten the ears, pinch them and sew them onto the head, on either side at rounds 30–32.

Antlers (make 2)

First piece

Round 1: using yarn C and a 2.5mm (UK 12/13, US 1/2) hook, 10 dc in an adjustable ring (10 sts).
Round 2: *1 dc, 2 dc in next st*, five times, stuff gently as you go (15 sts).
Rounds 3–6: 1 dc in each st (15 sts).
Round 7: *1 dc, dc2tog*, five times (10 sts).
Rounds 8–22: 1 dc in each st (10 sts).
Fasten off, leaving an end for sewing. Stuff.

Second piece

Round 1: using yarn C and a 2.5mm (UK 12/13, US 1/2) hook, 10 dc in an adjustable ring (10 sts).
Rounds 2–6: 1 dc in each st (10 sts).
Fasten off, leaving an end for sewing.
Stuff. Position and sew onto the first piece (see picture).

Third piece

Round 1: using yarn C and a 2.5mm (UK 12/13, US 1/2) hook, 10 dc in an adjustable ring (10 sts).
Rounds 2–4: 1 dc in each st (10 sts).
Fasten off, leaving an end for sewing.
Stuff. Position and sew onto first piece (see picture).

Sew the antler to the head on either side, diagonally below the ears, over rounds 34–36, with 11 sts in between.

Winter hat

The hat is crocheted in rows.

Row 1: using yarn F and a 2.5mm (UK 12/13, US 1/2) hook, ch 14, plus 1 ch to turn (14 sts).

Row 2: starting in the second ch from the hook, work 14 dc in bl, 1 ch to turn (14 sts).

Rows 3–23: 14 dc in bl, 1 ch to turn (14 sts).

Fasten off, leaving an end for sewing. Fold together, sew the sides together. Form the top of the hat by weaving the yarn in a zigzag pattern through the top edge of the hat. Then pull the yarn to close the hat.

Using yarn B, make a small pompom about 2.5cm (1in) in diameter. Sew the pompom onto the hat. Sew the hat onto the head. Sew the head onto the neck.

Beatrice Baby Bunny

Beatrice likes to scratch up golf courses and play hide and seek in green grass fields. Each night she collects the golf balls, working on her big dream: having a gigantic ball pool!

You will need

– Basic kit (see page 8)

– 2mm (UK 14, US 0) crochet hook

– Yarn:

• 4 balls of 4-ply (fingering), 100% cotton, 50g/1¾oz/160m/175yd. I used Hobbii Rainbow Cotton 8/4 in powder rose 063 (A), nude 003 (B), natural white 002 (C) and old rose 046 (D)

– Dark brown embroidery thread

I am 18cm (7in) tall,
including my ears

Legs and lower body

Start with the first leg.

Round 1: using yarn A and a 2mm (UK 14, US 0) hook, 8 dc in an adjustable ring (8 sts).

Close the ring with a sl st, ch 1.

Round 2: 1 dc in the back loop of each st (8 sts).

Round 3: *3 dc, 2 dc in next st*, twice (10 sts).

Round 4: *4 dc, 2 dc in next st*, twice (12 sts).

Round 5: *5 dc, 2 dc in next st*, twice (14 sts).

Round 6: 1 dc in each st (14 sts).

Fasten off. Crochet the second leg, but do not fasten off.

Round 7: join the two legs as follows: ch 4 at the end of the second leg, 14 dc (one in every stitch of the leg), ch 4, 14 dc in the second leg (4 + 14 + 4 + 14 = 36 sts). See page 15 for technique.

Round 8: 1 dc in each st (36 sts).

Round 9: *8 dc, 2 dc in next st*, three times, 9 dc (39 sts).

Round 10: 10 dc, 2 dc in next st, 9 dc, 2 dc in next st, 8 dc, 2 dc in next st, 9 dc (42 sts).

Round 11: 11 dc, 2 dc in next st, *9 dc, 2 dc in next st*, twice, 10 dc (45 sts).

Round 12: 11 dc, 2 dc in next st, *10 dc, 2 dc in next st*, twice, 11 dc (48 sts).

Rounds 13–23: 1 dc in each st (48 sts).

Round 24: 14 dc, dc2tog, 5 dc, dc2tog, *6 dc, dc2tog*, twice, 9 dc (44 sts).

Round 25: change to yarn B, 1 dc in each st (44 sts).

Stitch up the hole between the two legs and start stuffing the legs and lower body.

Round 26: 13 dc, dc2tog, 20 dc, dc2tog, 7 dc (42 sts).

Round 27: 1 dc in each st (42 sts).

Round 28: *5 dc, dc2tog*, six times (36 sts).

Round 29: 1 dc in each st (36 sts).

Round 30: *4 dc, dc2tog*, six times (30 sts).

Round 31: *3 dc, dc2tog*, six times (24 sts).

Round 32: *2 dc, dc2tog*, six times (18 sts).

Fasten off.

Stuff the legs and body firmly.

Head

Round 1: using yarn B and a 2mm (UK 14, US 0) hook, 6 dc in an adjustable ring (6 sts).
Round 2: 2 dc in each st (12 sts).
Round 3: *1 dc, 2 dc in next st*, six times (18 sts).
Round 4: *2 dc, 2 dc in next st*, six times (24 sts).
Round 5: *3 dc, 2 dc in next st*, six times (30 sts).
Round 6: *4 dc, 2 dc in next st*, six times (36 sts).
Round 7: 1 dc in each st (36 sts).
Round 8: *5 dc, 2 dc in next st*, six times (42 sts).
Rounds 9–14: 1 dc in each st (42 sts).
Round 15: *6 dc, 2 dc in next st*, six times (48 sts).
Round 16: *7 dc, 2 dc in next st*, six times (54 sts).
Round 17: *8 dc, 2 dc in next st*, six times (60 sts).
Rounds 18 and 19: 1 dc in each st (60 sts).
Round 20: *8 dc, dc2tog*, six times (54 sts).
Round 21: *7 dc, dc2tog*, six times (48 sts).
Round 22: *6 dc, dc2tog*, six times (42 sts).
Round 23: *5 dc, dc2tog*, six times (36 sts).
Round 24: *4 dc, dc2tog*, six times (30 sts).
Round 25: *3 dc, dc2tog*, six times (24 sts).
Round 26: *2 dc, dc2tog*, six times (18 sts).
Fasten off, leaving an end for sewing. Stuff the head and neck firmly.
Embroider the eyes around rounds 17 and 18, 10 sts apart. Embroider the snout on round 18.

Arms (make 2)

Round 1: using yarn B and a 2mm (UK 14, US 0) hook, 5 dc in an adjustable ring (5 sts).
Round 2: 2 dc in each st (10 sts).
Rounds 3–13: 1 dc in each st (10 sts).
Fasten off, leaving an end for sewing.
Gently stuff the front of the arms. Sew the arms onto the body on either side at round 29.

Tail

Round 1: using yarn A and a 2mm (UK 14, US 0) hook, 6 dc in an adjustable ring (6 sts).
Round 2: 2 dc in each st (12 sts).
Round 3: 1 dc in each st (12 sts).
Round 4: *dc2tog*, six times (6 sts).
Fasten off, leaving an end for sewing the tail to the body. Sew the tail to the body centred between the legs across rounds 10–12. Stuff the tail gently before closing the seam.

Cheeks (make 2)

Round 1: using yarn D and a 2mm (UK 14, US 0) hook, 7 dc in an adjustable ring (7 sts).
Fasten off, using the invisible finish, weave in the ends and glue the cheeks onto the face, diagonally below the eyes (see picture for position). See page 14 for the invisible finish technique.

Bow

Step 1: using yarn C and a 2mm (UK 14, US 0) hook, ch 4 (4 sts).
Step 2: 3 dtr in the fourth chain.
Step 3: ch 3.
Step 4: sl st in the first chain you've created (same as you've made the 3 dtr in).

You have now finished the first half of the bow.
Do not cut the yarn, repeat steps 1–4.
Pull the yarn tight to make the hole as small as possible, wrap the yarn around it five times and knot it at the back of the bow, leaving an end to sew the bow onto the head.

Ears

Round 1: using yarn B and a 2mm (UK 14, US 0) hook, 6 dc in an adjustable ring (6 sts).
Round 2: 1 dc in each st (6 sts).
Round 3: 2 dc in each st (12 sts).
Round 4: 1 dc in each st (12 sts).
Round 5: *1 dc, 2 dc in next st*, six times (18 sts).
Round 6: 1 dc in each st (18 sts).
Round 7: *3 dc, 2 dc in next st*, four times, 2 dc (22 sts).
Rounds 8–11: 1 dc in each st (22 sts).
Round 12: *3 dc, dc2tog in next st*, four times, 2 dc (18 sts).
Round 13: 1 dc in each st (18 sts).
Round 14: *2 dc, dc2tog in next st*, four times, 2 dc (14 sts).
Rounds 15 and 16: 1 dc in each st (14 sts).
Round 17: *1 dc, dc2tog in next st*, four times, 2 dc (10 sts).
Rounds 18 and 19: 1 dc in each st (10 sts).
Fasten off, leaving a tail for sewing. The ears are not stuffed. Flatten the ears and sew onto the head on either side across rounds 9 on the top of the head with 17 stitches between the ears. Sew the head onto the body.

Dungaree straps

Step 1: using yarn A and a 2mm (UK 14, US 0) hook, ch 23, end with a sl st, leaving an end for sewing. Sew the straps onto the trousers between rounds 24 and 25.
Step 2: embroider a few times over the knots on the front to create the effect of a button.

Puck Pugsie

Puck is very fond of yoga; he knows at least 20 different yoga positions. His favourite positions are 'downward facing dog' and 'extended puppy pose'. Next to yoga, he is very fond of sleeping. With his warm onesie and memory foam travel pillow, he is always ready for bed, whenever, wherever. He snores, but it is a cute snore.

You will need

- **Basic kit** **(see page 8)**
- **2mm (UK 14, US 0) crochet hook**
- **Yarn:**
  - 6 balls of 4-ply (fingering), 100% cotton, 50g/1¾oz/170m/186yd. I used Annell Cotton 8 in ecru 56 (A), dark grey 58 (B), old pink 51 (C) and Scheepjes Organicon in hickory 240 (D), deep sleep 256 (E) and soft sky 216 (F)
- **Dark brown embroidery thread**
- **Light brown felt**

I am 17cm (6¾in) tall

Legs and lower body

Start with the first leg.
Round 1: using yarn A and a 2mm (UK 14, US 0) hook, 6 dc in an adjustable ring (6 sts). Close the ring with a sl st, 1 ch.
Round 2: 2 dc in each st (12 sts).
Round 3: 1 dc in back loop of each st (12 sts).
Round 4: 1 dc in each st (12 sts).
Round 5: *1 dc, 2 dc in next st*, six times (18 sts).
Round 6: 1 dc in each st (18 sts).
Round 7: change to yarn B, 1 dc in each st (18 sts).
Round 8: *2 dc, 2 dc in next st*, six times (24 sts).
Rounds 9 and 10: 1 dc in each st (24 sts).
Fasten off. Crochet the second leg, but do not fasten off.
Round 11: join the two legs as follows: ch 6 at the end of the second leg, 24 dc (one in every stitch of the leg), ch 6, 24 dc in the second leg (6 + 24 + 6 + 24 = 60 sts).
Rounds 12–17: 1 dc in each st (60 sts).
Round 18: 1 dc in the back loop of each st (60 sts).
Rounds 19–33: 1 dc in each st (60 sts).
Fasten off. Stitch up the hole between the two legs and stuff the legs and body firmly.

Head

Round 1: using yarn A and a 2mm (UK 14, US 0) hook, 6 dc in an adjustable ring (6 sts).
Round 2: 2 dc in each st (12 sts).
Round 3: *1 dc, 2 dc in next st*, six times (18 sts).
Round 4: *2 dc, 2 dc in next st*, six times (24 sts).
Round 5: *3 dc, 2 dc in next st*, six times (30 sts).
Round 6: *4 dc, 2 dc in next st*, six times (36 sts).
Round 7: *5 dc, 2 dc in next st*, six times (42 sts).
Round 8: *6 dc, 2 dc in next st*, six times (48 sts).
Round 9: *7 dc, 2 dc in next st*, six times (54 sts).
Round 10: *8 dc, 2 dc in next st*, six times (60 sts).
Round 11: *9 dc, 2 dc in next st*, six times (66 sts).
Rounds 12–22: 1 dc in each st (66 sts).
Round 23: *9 dc, dc2tog*, six times (60 sts).
Fasten off, leaving an end for sewing. Stuff the head firmly.
Embroider the eyes over rounds 17 and 18, 11 sts apart.

Muzzle

Step 1: cut out the muzzle template in light brown felt.
Step 2: using dark brown embroidery thread, embroider the snout on the felt.
Step 3: glue the muzzle onto the head, between the eyes, across rounds 17–20.

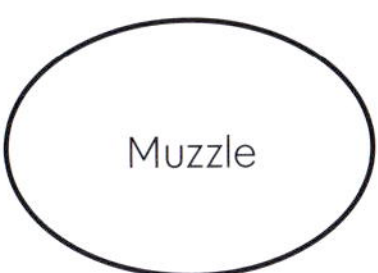

Cheeks (make 2)

Round 1: using yarn C and a 2mm (UK 14, US 0) hook, 8 dc in an adjustable ring (8 sts).
Fasten off, using the invisible finish, weave in the ends and glue the cheeks onto the face, diagonally below the eyes (see picture for position). See page 14 for the invisible finish technique.

Ears (make 2)

Round 1: using yarn D and a 2mm (UK 14, US 0) hook, 6 dc in an adjustable ring (6 sts).
Round 2: 2 dc in each st (12 sts).
Rounds 3 and 4: 1 dc in each st (12 sts).
Round 5: *1 dc, 2 dc in next st*, six times (18 sts).
Rounds 6–8: 1 dc in each st (18 sts).
Round 9: *3 dc, dc2tog*, three times, 1 dc, dc2tog (14 sts).
Rounds 10 and 11: 1 dc in each st (14 sts).
Round 12: *1 dc, dc2tog*, four times, 2 dc (10 sts).
Round 13: 1 dc in each st (10 sts).
Fasten off, leaving an end for sewing. Do not stuff the ears. Flatten the ears, sew onto the head on either side across rounds 6–16 on the top of the head with 10 sts in between the ears. Sew the head onto the body.

Arms (make 2)

Round 1: using yarn A and a 2mm (UK 14, US 0) hook, 5 dc in an adjustable ring (5 sts).
Round 2: 2 dc in each st (10 sts).
Rounds 3–5: 1 dc in each st (10 sts).
Round 6: change to yarn B, 1 dc in each st (10 sts).
Rounds 7–15: 1 dc in each st (10 sts).
Fasten off, leaving an end for sewing.
Gently stuff the front of the arms.
Sew the arms onto the body, leaning inwards, on either side at rounds 28–31. See picture for position.

Tail

The tail is crocheted in rows.
Row 1: using yarn A and a 2mm (UK 14, US 0) hook, ch 8 (8 sts).
Row 2: starting in the second ch from the hook, 2 dc in each st (14 sts).
Fasten off, leaving an end for sewing.
Sew the tail to the back of the body at round 17.

Pyjama collar

The collar is crocheted in rows, not in rounds, using v-shaped dc.
Row 1: using yarn B and a 2mm (UK 14, US 0) hook, ch 66, plus 1 ch to turn (66 sts).
Rows 2–4: 66 dc, 1 ch to turn (66 sts).
Row 5: sl st in every st (66 sts).
Fasten off, place the collar with the v-shaped edge on top, on the body.
Sew the bottom side onto the body on round 33 so that the collar itself reaches a bit higher, just below the muzzle.
Sew the ends of the collar together.
Weave in the ends.

Pillow

The pillow is crocheted in rows and the x-shaped dc. Make sure your ends are always at the wrong side of the work. When changing colour at the other side of the work, this means that you will have to cut the yarn and sew it manually to the wrong side. You can then tie together these ends.
Change colour by joining in the new colour during the final step of the last stitch in the old colour.
When you must change colour in the next row, as in row 8, then you'll have to change colour in the final turning stitch of the previous round. See page 15 for technique.

Front and back piece

Row 1: using yarn E and a 2mm (UK 14, US 0) hook, ch 18, plus 1 ch to turn (18 sts).
Row 2: 9 dc, change to yarn F, 9 dc, 1 ch to turn (18 sts).
Row 3: 9 dc, change to yarn E, 9 dc, 1 ch to turn (18 sts).
Rows 4–7: repeat rows 2 and 3 twice more.
Row 8: change to yarn F, 9 dc, change to yarn E, 9 dc, 1 ch to turn (18 sts).
Row 9: 9 dc, change to yarn F, 9 dc, 1 ch to turn (18 sts).
Rows 10–13: repeat rows 8 and 9 twice more.
Row 14: repeat row 8.
Row 15: change to yarn F, 1 dc in each st (18 sts).
Fasten off. Weave in the ends.

Crochet the second piece. Place the wrong sides of the pieces against each other and connect them using yarn E with v-shaped dc around the edge (see picture). Crochet 3 dc in the same st in each corner to make smooth curves. I've crocheted 18 dc on each long side of the pillow, and 13 dc on each short side.

Connect three sides, stuff the pillow gently and connect the last side. End with a sl st, leaving a long end for sewing the pillow under Puck's arm.

Polly Penguin

Polly can't do without her frappés with caramel and chocolate sprinkles. She also can't do without her pink bodywarmer, even though she's from Australia and it is way too hot for bodywarmers there.

You will need

- **Basic kit (see page 8)**
- **2mm (UK 14, US 0) crochet hook**
- **Yarn:**
  - 2 balls of 4-ply (fingering), 100% cotton, 50g/1¾oz/175m/191yd. I used Annell Cotton 8 in dark grey 58 (A) and old pink 51 (B)
  - 2 balls of 5-ply (sport), 78% cotton, 22% acrylic, 50g/1¾oz/130m/142yd. I used Scheepjes Stone Washed in larimar 828 (C) and pink quartzite 821 (D)
- **Embroidery thread in black and pink**
- **Felt in white and black**

I am 16cm (6¼in) tall

Legs and lower body

Start with the first leg.

Round 1: using yarn A and a 2mm (UK 14, US 0) hook, 8 dc in an adjustable ring (8 sts).

Close the ring with a sl st, ch 1.

Round 2: 1 dc in the back loop of each st (8 sts).

Round 3: *3 dc, 2 dc in next st*, twice (10 sts).

Round 4: *4 dc, 2 dc in next st*, twice (12 sts).

Round 5: *5 dc, 2 dc in next st*, twice (14 sts).

Round 6: 1 dc in each st (14 sts).

Fasten off. Crochet the second leg, but do not fasten off.

Round 7: join the two legs as follows: ch 4 at the end of the second leg, 14 dc (one in every stitch of the leg), ch 4, 14 dc in the second leg (4 + 14 + 4 + 14 = 36 sts). See page 15 for technique.

Round 8: 1 dc in each st (36 sts).

Round 9: *8 dc, 2 dc in next st*, three times, 9 dc (39 sts).

Round 10: 10 dc, 2 dc in next st, 9 dc, 2 dc in next st, 8 dc, 2 dc in next st, 9 dc (42 sts).

You'll now start crocheting the sweater in v-shaped dc. In round 11, crochet through both loops, but for rounds 12–26 crochet only through the back loop.

Round 11: changing to yarn C, 1 dc in each st (42 sts).

Rounds 12–22: changing to yarn D, 1 dc in bl of each st (42 sts).

Continue in a stripe pattern, alternating between 1 round in yarn C and 1 round in yarn D, crocheting only in the back loop.

Stitch up the hole between the two legs and start stuffing the legs and lower body.

Round 23: change to yarn C, *5 dc, dc2tog*, six times (36 sts).

Round 24: change to yarn D, 1 dc in each st (36 sts).

Round 25: change to yarn C, *4 dc, dc2tog*, six times (30 sts).

Fasten off, weave in the end. Stuff the body firmly.

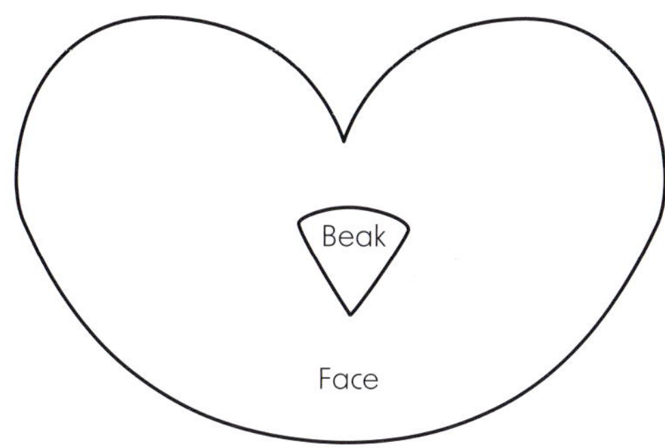

Head

Round 1: using yarn A and a 2mm (UK 14, US 0) hook, 6 dc in an adjustable ring (6 sts).
Round 2: 2 dc in each st (12 sts).
Round 3: *1 dc, 2 dc in next st*, six times (18 sts).
Round 4: *2 dc, 2 dc in next st*, six times (24 sts).
Round 5: *3 dc, 2 dc in next st*, six times (30 sts).
Round 6: *4 dc, 2 dc in next st*, six times (36 sts).
Round 7: *5 dc, 2 dc in next st*, six times (42 sts).
Round 8: *6 dc, 2 dc in next st*, six times (48 sts).
Rounds 9–19: 1 dc in each st (48 sts).
Round 20: *6 dc, dc2tog*, six times (42 sts).
Round 21: 1 dc in each st (42 sts).
Round 22: *5 dc, dc2tog*, six times (36 sts).
Round 23: *4 dc, dc2tog*, six times (30 sts).
Fasten off, leaving an end for sewing. Stuff the head firmly.

Face

Step 1: cut out the face in white felt and cut out the beak in black felt.
Step 2: using black embroidery thread, embroider the eyes on the white felt.
Step 3: glue the beak onto the face (see picture for position).
Step 4: embroider the cheeks onto the white felt.
Step 5: glue the face onto the head across rounds 9–21.
Sew the head onto the body.

Flippers (make 2)

Round 1: using yarn A and a 2mm (UK 14, US 0) hook, 6 dc in an adjustable ring (6 sts).
Round 2: 1 dc in each st (6 sts).
Round 3: 2 dc in each st (12 sts).
Round 4: 1 dc in each st (12 sts).
Round 5: *1 dc, 2 dc in next st*, six times (18 sts).
Rounds 6–9: 1 dc in each sts (18 sts).
Round 10: *3 dc, dc2tog*, three times, 1 dc, dc2tog (14 sts).
Rounds 11 and 12: 1 dc in each st (14 sts).
Round 13: change to yarn D, crochet in v-shaped dc and through both loops, 1 dc in each st (14 sts).
Round 14: change to yarn C, crochet in v-shaped dc and through the back loop only, 1 dc in each st (14 sts).
Fasten off, leaving an end for sewing.
Do not stuff the flippers.
Sew the flippers onto the body on either side at round 23.

Tail

Round 1: using yarn A and a 2mm (UK 14, US 0) hook, 6 dc in an adjustable ring (6 sts).
Round 2: 1 dc in each st (6 sts).
Round 3: 2 dc in each st (12 sts).
Rounds 4–6: 1 dc in each st (12 sts).
Fasten off, leaving an end for sewing.
Do not stuff the tail.
Sew the tail onto the centre of the body in the back on round 11.

Bodywarmer

The bodywarmer is crocheted in rows.

Row 1: using yarn B and a 2mm (UK 14, US 0) hook, ch 36, plus 2 ch to turn (36 sts).

Row 2: starting in the third ch from the hook, 36 htr, 2 ch to turn (36 sts).

Row 3: 3 htr, 7 ch, skip next 7 sts, 16 htr, 7 ch, skip next 7 sts, 3 htr, 2 ch to turn (36 sts).

Rows 4–12: 1 htr in each st, 2 ch to turn (36 sts).

Row 13: 1 htr in each st, 1 ch to turn (36 sts).

Row 14: starting in the second stitch on the hoop, 1 sl st in each st (36 sts).

Fasten off. Weave in the ends.

Put the bodywarmer on Polly.

Bodywarmer collar

The collar is crocheted in rows.

Row 1: using yarn C and a 2mm (UK 14, US 0) hook, ch 36, plus 2 ch to turn (36 sts).

Row 2: starting in the third ch from the hook, 1 htr in each st, 1 ch to turn (36 sts).

Row 3: 1 sl st in each st (36 sts).

Fasten off. Sew the ends together (while around the neck)

Ricky Raccoon

Ricky looks like a little ninja but is in fact a pacifist. He doesn't believe in violence, but in random acts of kindness; he turns off bicycle lights in the bike parking, so that cyclists can cycle home safely at the end of the day and leaves sweet notes under windscreen wipers just to get people smiling. He is also a firm believer of the benefits of outdoor swimming, so he always has his towel with him.

You will need

- **Basic kit (see page 8)**
- **2mm (UK 14, US 0) crochet hook**
- **Yarn:**
  - 6 balls of 4-ply (fingering), 100% cotton, 50g/1¾oz/170m/186yd. I used Annell Cotton 8 in reddish brown 30 (A) and ecru 56 (B); Scheepjes Organicon in cornflower blue 253 (C), oxygen 219 (D) and hickory 240 (E); and Annell Cotton 8 in old pink 51 (F)
- **2 safety eyes, 8mm (5⁄16in)**
- **Dark brown embroidery thread**
- **Dark brown felt**

I am 15cm (6in) tall

Legs and lower body

Start with the first leg.

Round 1: using yarn A and a 2mm (UK 14, US 0) hook, 8 dc in an adjustable ring (8 sts).

Close the ring with a sl st, ch 1.

Round 2: 1 dc in the back loop of each st (8 sts).

Round 3: *3 dc, 2 dc in next st*, twice (10 sts).

Round 4: *4 dc, 2 dc in next st*, twice (12 sts).

Round 5: *5 dc, 2 dc in next st*, twice (14 sts).

Round 6: change to yarn D, 1 dc in each st (14 sts).

Fasten off. Crochet the second leg, but do not fasten off.

Round 7: join the two legs as follows: ch 4 at the end of the second leg, 14 dc (one in every stitch of the leg), ch 4, 14 dc in the second leg (4 + 14 + 4 + 14 = 36 sts). See page 15 for technique.

Round 8: change to yarn C, 1 dc in each st (36 sts).

Round 9: *8 dc, 2 dc in next st*, three times, 9 dc (39 sts).

Round 10: change to yarn D, 10 dc, 2 dc in next st, 9 dc, 2 dc in next st, 8 dc, 2 dc in next st, 9 dc (42 sts).

Round 11: 11 dc, 2 dc in next st, *9 dc, 2 dc in next st*, twice, 10 dc (45 sts).

Round 12: change to yarn C, 11 dc, 2 dc in next st, *10 dc, 2 dc in next st*, twice, 11 dc (48 sts).

Round 13: 1 dc in each st (48 sts).

Rounds 14 and 15: change to yarn D, 1 dc in each st (48 sts).

Rounds 16–20: change to yarn A, 1 dc in each st (48 sts).

Round 21: 14 dc, dc2tog, 5 dc, dc2tog, *6 dc, dc2tog*, twice, 9 dc (44 sts).

Round 22: 1 dc in each st (44 sts).
Stitch up the hole between the two legs and start stuffing the legs and lower body.
Round 23: 13 dc, dc2tog, 20 dc, dc2tog, 7 dc (42 sts).
Round 24: 1 dc in each st (42 sts).
Round 25: *5 dc, dc2tog*, six times (36 sts).
Round 26: *4 dc, dc2tog*, six times (30 sts).
Round 27: 1 dc in each st (30 sts).
Round 28: *3 dc, dc2tog*, six times (24 sts).
Round 29: *2 dc, dc2tog*, six times (18 sts).
Fasten off.
Stuff the legs and body firmly. Weave in the ends.

Drawstring

Using yarn A and a 2mm (UK 14, US 0) hook, chain 64.
Fasten off. Glue the drawstring on the top row of the shorts, but leave the ends free, so that you can knot them together.

Head

Change colour by joining in the new colour during the final step of the last stitch in the old colour. See page 15 for technique.

Round 1: using yarn A and a 2mm (UK 14, US 0) hook, 6 dc in an adjustable ring (6 sts).
Round 2: 2 dc in each st (12 sts).
Round 3: *1 dc, 2 dc in next st*, six times (18 sts).
Round 4: *2 dc, 2 dc in next st*, six times (24 sts).
Round 5: *3 dc, 2 dc in next st*, six times (30 sts).
Round 6: *4 dc, 2 dc in next st*, six times (36 sts).
Round 7: *5 dc, 2 dc in next st*, six times (42 sts).
Round 8: *6 dc, 2 dc in next st*, six times (48 sts).
Round 9: 1 dc in each st (48 sts).
Round 10: *7 dc, 2 dc in next st*, six times (54 sts).
Round 11: 1 dc in each st (54 sts).
Round 12: 11 dc, change to yarn B, 10 dc, change to yarn A, 5 dc, change to yarn B, 10 dc, change to yarn A, 18 dc (54 sts).
Round 13: 10 dc, change to yarn B, 12 dc, change to yarn A, 3 dc, change to yarn B, 12 dc, change to yarn A, 17 dc (54 sts).
Rounds 14 and 15: 10 dc, change to yarn B, 27 dc, change to yarn A, 17 dc (54 sts).
Rounds 16–18: 11 dc, change to yarn B, 25 dc, change to yarn A, 18 dc (54 sts).
Round 19: 7 dc, dc2tog, 2 dc, change to yarn B, 5 dc, dc2tog, 7 dc, dc2tog, 6 dc, dc2tog, 1 dc, change to yarn A, 7 dc, dc2tog, 7 dc, dc2tog (48 sts).
Round 20: 10 dc, change to yarn B, 22 dc, change to yarn A, 16 dc (48 sts).
Round 21: 6 dc, dc2tog, 2 dc, change to yarn B, 4 dc, dc2tog, 6 dc, dc2tog, 5 dc, dc2tog, 1 dc, change to yarn A, 6 dc, dc2tog, 6 dc, dc2tog (42 sts).
Round 22: 5 dc, dc2tog, 2 dc, change to yarn B, 3 dc, dc2tog, 5 dc, dc2tog, 4 dc, dc2tog, 1 dc, change to yarn A, 5 dc, dc2tog, 5 dc, dc2tog (36 sts).
Round 23: 4 dc, dc2tog, 2 dc, change to yarn B, 2 dc, dc2tog, 4 dc, dc2tog, 3 dc, dc2tog, 1 dc, change to yarn A, 4 dc, dc2tog, 4 dc, dc2tog (30 sts).
Round 24: 3 dc, dc2tog, 3 dc, change to yarn B, *dc2tog, 3 dc*, twice, dc2tog, change to yarn A, *3 dc, dc2tog*, twice (24 sts).
Round 25: *2 dc, dc2tog*, six times (18 sts).
Fasten off, leaving an end for sewing the head onto the body (after you have attached the ears and cheeks). Stuff firmly.

Using the dark brown felt and the template below, cut out the mask.

Insert the safety eyes through the mask (position is marked on the template), use a tiny hole punch if necessary, and attach the safety eyes between rounds 15 and 16 with 11 sts in between.

Glue the felt to the head.

Using dark brown thread, embroider the snout centrally between the eyes, 1 round below the bottom side of the mask, on rounds 17 and 18.

Ears (make 2)

Round 1: using yarn B and a 2mm (UK 14, US 0) hook, 6 dc in an adjustable ring (6 sts).
Round 2: 1 dc in each st (6 sts).
Round 3: change to yarn A, 2 dc in each st (12 sts).
Round 4: 1 dc in each st (12 sts).
Round 5: *1 dc, 2 dc in next st*, six times (18 sts).
Round 6: 1 dc in each st (18 sts).
Round 7: *2 dc, 2 dc in next st*, six times (24 sts).
Round 8: 1 dc in each st (24 sts).
Round 9: *2 dc, dc2tog in next st*, six times (18 sts).

Fasten off, leaving an end for sewing. Do not stuff the ears. Before folding the ears, embroider the dark brown stripes on one side. (The back of the ear does not have embroidery.)

Flatten and pinch the ears, sew onto the head on either side across rounds 6–13 on the top of the head with 10 sts in between the ears.

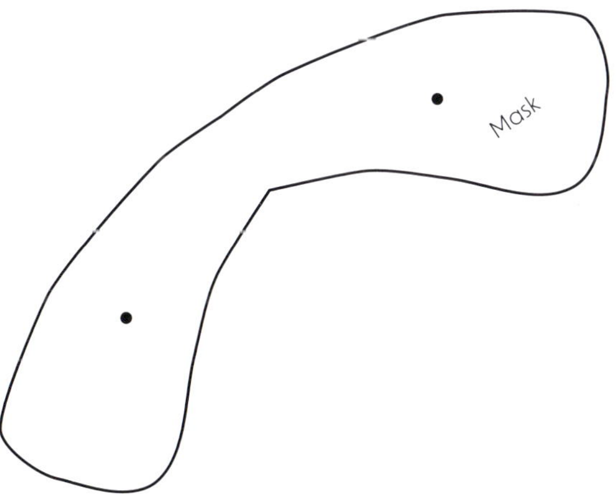

Tail

Round 1: using yarn E and a 2mm (UK 14, US 0) hook, 4 dc in an adjustable ring (4 sts).
Round 2: *1 dc, 2 dc in next st*, twice (6 sts).
Round 3: *2 dc, 2 dc in next st*, twice (8 sts).
Round 4: *1 dc, 2 dc in next st*, four times (12 sts).
Round 5: *5 dc, 2 dc in next st*, twice (14 sts).
Round 6: change to yarn A, *6 dc, 2 dc in next st*, twice (16 sts).
Round 7: *7 dc, 2 dc in next st*, twice (18 sts).
Rounds 8 and 9: change to yarn E, 1 dc in each st (18 sts).
Rounds 10 and 11: change to yarn A, 1 dc in each st (18 sts).
Round 12: change to yarn E, 1 dc in each st (18 sts).
Round 13: *7 dc, dc2tog*, twice (16 sts).
Round 14: change to yarn A, *6 dc, dc2tog*, twice (14 sts).
Round 15: *5 dc, dc2tog*, twice (12 sts).
Round 16: change to yarn E, 1 dc in each st (12 sts).
Round 17: *4 dc, dc2tog*, twice (10 sts).
Round 18: change to yarn A, *3 dc, dc2tog*, twice (8 sts).
Fasten off, leaving an end for sewing.
Gently stuff the tail.
Sew the tail to the back of the body at round 13.

Arms (make 2)

Round 1: using yarn A and a 2mm (UK 14, US 0) hook, 5 dc in an adjustable ring (5 sts).
Round 2: 2 dc in each st (10 sts).
Rounds 3–13: 1 dc in each st (10 sts).
Fasten off, leaving an end for sewing.
Gently stuff the front of the arms. Sew the arms onto the body on either side at round 27.

Cheeks (make 2)

Round 1: using yarn F and a 2mm (UK 14, US 0) hook, 5 dc in an adjustable ring (5 sts).
Fasten off with an invisible finish, weave in the ends.
Glue the cheeks onto the mask, diagonally below the eyes (see picture for position).

Swimming towel

The towel is crocheted in rows and in v-shaped dc.
Row 1: using yarn F and a 2mm (UK 14, US 0) hook, ch 20, plus 1 ch to turn (20 sts).
Rows 2–28: 1 dc in each st (20 sts).
Fasten off. Weave in the ends.
Roll up the towel, tie a piece of yarn around it, or glue the ends of the towel to keep it rolled up.
Sew the towel under Ricky's arm.

Cato Cat

Cato adores fish. She even has a designer bag in the shape of a fish and calls it her little Nemo. The bag does not look very big, but it has lots of compartments filled with Cato's indispensable items like crabsticks, her pink travel litter box, her glitter pens and the one book she can't do without: *The Rainbow Fish* by Marcus Pfister.

You will need

- **Basic kit (see page 8)**
- **2mm (UK 14, US 0) crochet hook**
- **Yarn:**
  - 6 balls of 4-ply (fingering), 100% cotton, 50g/1¾oz/170m/186yd. I used Scheepjes Organicon in oxygen 219 (A), ashen mink 201 (B), bright ocean 215 (C), pink petunia 249 (D), happy sunflower 238 (E) and bluebell 255 (F)
- **2 safety eyes, 7mm (¼in)**
- **Dark brown embroidery thread**
- **Felt in white and dark brown**

I am 16cm (6¼in) tall

Patchy leg and lower body

Change colour by joining in the new colour during the final step of the last stitch in the old colour. See page 15 for technique.

Start with the first leg.

Round 1: using yarn B and a 2mm (UK 14, US 0) hook, 8 dc in an adjustable ring (8 sts).

Close the ring with a sl st, ch 1.

Round 2: 1 dc in the back loop of each st (8 sts).

Round 3: 1 dc, change to yarn A, 2 dc, 2 dc in next st, change to yarn B, 3 dc, 2 dc in next st (10 sts).

Round 4: 1 dc, change to yarn A, 3 dc, 2 dc in next st, 1 dc, change to yarn B, 3 dc, 2 dc in next st (12 sts).

Round 5: 1 dc, change to yarn A, 4 dc, 2 dc in next st, change to yarn B, 5 dc, 2 dc in next st (14 sts).

Round 6: change to yarn A, 11 dc (do not finish this round, but fasten off here) (14 sts).

Crochet the second leg, this time only with yarn A, but do not fasten off.

Second leg and upper body

Round 1: using yarn A and a 2mm (UK 14, US 0) hook, 8 dc in an adjustable ring (8 sts).

Close the ring with a sl st, ch 1.

Round 2: 1 dc in the back loop of each st (8 sts).

Round 3: *3 dc, 2 dc in next st*, twice (10 sts).

Round 4: *4 dc, 2 dc in next st*, twice (12 sts).

Round 5: *5 dc, 2 dc in next st*, twice (14 sts).

Round 6: 1 dc in each st (14 sts).

Round 7: join the two legs as follows: ch 4 at the end of the second leg, 14 dc (one in every stitch of the leg), ch 4, 14 dc in the second leg (4 + 14 + 4 + 14 = 36 sts). See page 15 for technique.

Round 8: 1 dc in each st (36 sts).

Round 9: *8 dc, 2 dc in next st*, three times, 9 dc (39 sts).

Round 10: 10 dc, 2 dc in next st, 9 dc, 2 dc in next st, 8 dc, 2 dc in next st, 9 dc (42 sts).

Round 11: 11 dc, 2 dc in next st, *9 dc, 2 dc in next st*, twice, 10 dc (45 sts).

Round 12: 11 dc, 2 dc in next st, *10 dc, 2 dc in next st*, twice, 11 dc (48 sts).

Rounds 13–17: 1 dc in each st (48 sts).
Rounds 18–20: change to yarn C, 1 dc in each st (48 sts).
Round 21: 14 dc, dc2tog, 5 dc, dc2tog, *6 dc, dc2tog*, twice, 9 dc (44 sts).
Round 22: 1 dc in each st (44 sts).
Stitch up the hole between the two legs and start stuffing the legs and lower body.

Round 23: 13 dc, dc2tog, 20 dc, dc2tog, 7 dc (42 sts).
Round 24: 1 dc in each st (42 sts).
Round 25: *5 dc, dc2tog*, six times (36 sts).
Round 26: *4 dc, dc2tog*, six times (30 sts).
Round 27: 1 dc in each st (30 sts).
Round 28: *3 dc, dc2tog*, six times (24 sts).
Round 29: *2 dc, dc2tog*, six times (18 sts).
Fasten off.
Stuff the legs and body firmly. Weave in the ends.

Head

Round 1: using yarn A and a 2mm (UK 14, US 0) hook, 6 dc in an adjustable ring (6 sts).
Round 2: 2 dc in each st (12 sts).
Round 3: *1 dc, 2 dc in next st*, six times (18 sts).
Round 4: *2 dc, 2 dc in next st*, six times (24 sts).
Round 5: *3 dc, 2 dc in next st*, six times (30 sts).
Round 6: *4 dc, 2 dc in next st*, six times (36 sts).
Round 7: *5 dc, 2 dc in next st*, six times (42 sts).
Round 8: *6 dc, 2 dc in next st*, six times (48 sts).
Round 9: 1 dc in each st (48 sts).
Round 10: *7 dc, 2 dc in next st*, six times (54 sts).
Round 11: 24 dc, change to yarn B, 7 dc, change to yarn A, 23 dc (54 sts).
Round 12: 23 dc, change to yarn B, 9 dc, change to yarn A, 22 dc (54 sts).
Rounds 13–15: 22 dc, change to yarn B, 11 dc, change to yarn A, 21 dc (54 sts).
Round 16: 23 dc, change to yarn B, 10 dc, change to yarn A, 21 dc (54 sts).
Round 17: 24 dc, change to yarn B, 9 dc, change to yarn A, 21 dc (54 sts).
Round 18: 25 dc, change to yarn B, 8 dc, change to yarn A, 21 dc (54 sts).
Round 19: *7 dc, dc2tog*, six times (48 sts).
Round 20: 1 dc in each st (48 sts).
Round 21: *6 dc, dc2tog*, six times (42 sts).
Round 22: *5 dc, dc2tog st*, six times (36 sts).
Round 23: *4 dc, dc2tog st*, six times (30 sts).
Attach the safety eyes between rounds 15 and 16, with 11 sts in between.

Round 24: *3 dc, dc2tog st*, six times (24 sts).
Fasten off, leaving an end for sewing the head onto the body (after you have attached the ears and cheeks). Stuff firmly.
Using the dark brown felt and the template above, cut out the nose.
Glue the nose to the head. Using dark brown embroidery thread, embroider the mouth. With yarn D, embroider the cheeks (see picture for position).

Nose

Ears (make 1 in yarn A, 1 in yarn B)

Round 1: using yarn A or B and a 2mm (UK 14, US 0) hook, 6 dc in an adjustable ring (6 sts).
Round 2: *1 dc, 2 dc in next st*, three times (9 sts).
Round 3: *2 dc, 2 dc in next st*, three times (12 sts).
Round 4: 1 dc in each st (12 sts).
Round 5: *3 dc, 2 dc in next st*, three times (15 sts).
Round 6: *4 dc, 2 dc in next st*, three times (18 sts).
Round 7: *5 dc, 2 dc in next st*, three times (21 sts).
Round 8: *6 dc, 2 dc in next st*, three times (24 sts).
Fasten off, leaving an end for sewing. The ears are not stuffed. Flatten them and sew onto the head on either side across rounds 4–13 on the top of the head with 10 sts in between the ears.

Arms (make 2)

Fish

Round 1: using yarn A and a 2mm (UK 14, US 0) hook, 5 dc in an adjustable ring (5 sts).
Round 2: 2 dc in each st (10 sts).
Rounds 3–9: 1 dc in each st (10 sts).
Rounds 10–13: change to yarn C, 1 dc in each st (10 sts).
Fasten off, leaving an end to sew the arm onto the body.
Stuff the front of the arms gently. Sew the arms to the body on either side on round 29.
Using the white felt and the template above, cut out 17 little fish. Glue them on Cato's t-shirt after you have sewn the arms onto the body.

Tail

The tail is crocheted in rows.
Row 1: using yarn A and a 2mm (UK 14, US 0) hook, ch 16, plus 1 ch to turn (16 sts).
Row 2: 1 sl st in every st (16 sts).
Fasten off, leaving an end to sew the tail to the body. Sew the tail to the body centrally between the legs between rounds 13 and 14.

Fish bag

Round 1: using yarn E and a 2mm (UK 14, US 0) hook, 6 dc in an adjustable ring (6 sts).
Round 2: 2 dc in each st (12 sts).
Round 3: *1 dc, 2 dc in next st*, six times (18 sts).
Rounds 4–8: 1 dc in each st (18 sts).
Round 9: *1 dc, dc2tog in next st*, six times (12 sts).
Round 10: *dc2tog*, six times (6 sts).
Stuff the bag very gently.
Round 11: pinch the opening flat. Crochet the front and back together to close the fish.

From this point the bag is crocheted in rows instead of rounds. Ch 1, then 3 dc across both layers to close the opening (3 sts).
Row 1: ch 4, (1 tr, 3 dtr) in the first st, 3 dtr in the second st, (3 dtr, 1 tr) in the last st, ch 2, sl st into the last st (11 sts).
Fasten off, weave in the ends.

Bag handle

Using yarn E and a 2mm (UK 14, US 0) hook, ch 25 (25 sts).
Close the ring with a sl st. Sew the handle on the bag in the crease of the fish's tail, see picture.

Skirt

Round 1: using yarn F and a 2mm (UK 14, US 0) hook, ch 54 (54 sts).
Round 2: join into a ring with dc, 53 dc (54 sts).
Round 3: *8 dc, 2 dc in next st*, six times (60 sts).
Round 4: *9 dc, 2 dc in next st*, six times (66 sts).
Rounds 5 and 6: 1 dc in each st (66 sts).
Round 7: 1 sl st in each st (66 sts).
Fasten off with an invisible finish (see page 14).
Weave in the ends.

Skirt waistband

Join yarn F in round 1 of the skirt.
Round 1: 1 dc in each st (54 sts).
Round 2: sl st in each st (54 sts).
Fasten off with an invisible finish. Weave in the ends.

Stevie Snail

Stevie is a very mindful little fellow. Slowly he crosses the world, always on the lookout for tiny treasures like lost coins and cookie crumbs. He's also very stylish and a bit eccentric. He swears by his little sun hat, and his shell is decorated with happy African flowers that brighten up every day, even the rainy ones.

You will need

– Basic kit (see page 8)

– 2mm (UK 14, US 0) crochet hook

– Yarn:

• 7 balls of 4-ply (fingering), 100% cotton, 50g/1¾oz/170m/186yd. I used Scheepjes Organicon in ashen mink 201 (A), peach fuzz 208 (B), amaranth 245 (C), soft sky 216 (D), deep sleep 256 (E), broken almond 220 (F) and pink petunia 249 (G)

– 2 safety eyes, 5mm (3⁄16in)

– Dark brown embroidery thread

– Tweezers

I am 15cm (6in) long

Head and body

Round 1: using yarn A and a 2mm (UK 14, US 0) hook, 6 dc in an adjustable ring (6 sts).
Round 2: 2 dc in each st (12 sts).
Round 3: *1 dc, 2 dc in next st*, six times (18 sts).
Round 4: *2 dc, 2 dc in next st*, six times (24 sts).
Round 5: *3 dc, 2 dc in next st*, six times (30 sts).
Rounds 6–10: 1 dc in each st (30 sts).
Attach the safety eyes between rounds 6 and 7, between the eighth and ninth stitch and the twenty-third and twenty-fourth stitch, 14 stitches apart.
Round 11: 28 dc, dc2tog (29 sts).
Round 12: 1 dc in each st (29 sts).
Round 13: 27 dc, dc2tog (28 sts).
Round 14: 1 dc in each st (28 sts).
Stuff the head firmly but stuff the middle part of the body very gently while you continue. Use tweezers to put the stuffing in the tail section.
Round 15: 26 dc, dc2tog (27 sts).
Round 16: 1 dc in each st (27 sts).
Round 17: 25 dc, dc2tog (26 sts).
Round 18: 1 dc in each st (26 sts).
Round 19: 24 dc, dc2tog (25 sts).
Round 20: 1 dc in each st (25 sts).
Round 21: 23 dc, dc2tog (24 sts).
Round 22: 1 dc in each st (24 sts).
Round 23: 22 dc, dc2tog (23 sts).
Rounds 24 and 25: 1 dc in each st (23 sts).
Round 26: 21 dc, dc2tog (22 sts).
Rounds 27 and 28: 1 dc in each st (22 sts).
Round 29: 20 dc, dc2tog (21 sts).
Round 30: 1 dc in each st (21 sts).
Round 31: 19 dc, dc2tog (20 sts).
Round 32: 1 dc in each st (20 sts).
Round 33: 18 dc, dc2tog (19 sts).
Round 34: 1 dc in each st (19 sts).
Round 35: 17 dc, dc2tog (18 sts).
Round 36: 1 dc in each st (18 sts).
Round 37: 16 dc, dc2tog (17 sts).
Round 38: 1 dc in each st (17 sts).
Round 39: 15 dc, dc2tog (16 sts).
Round 40: 14 dc, dc2tog (15 sts).
Round 41: 13 dc, dc2tog (14 sts).
Round 42: 12 dc, dc2tog (13 sts).
Round 43: 11 dc, dc2tog (12 sts).
Round 44: 10 dc, dc2tog (11 sts).
Round 45: 9 dc, dc2tog (10 sts).
Round 46: 8 dc, dc2tog (9 sts).
Round 47: 7 dc, dc2tog (8 sts).
Round 48: 6 dc, dc2tog (7 sts).
Round 49: 5 dc, dc2tog (6 sts).
Fasten off, weave your yarn through the front loop of each st, and pull. Weave in the end.
With dark brown embroidery thread, embroider the mouth between rounds 2 and 3.
With yarn G, embroider the cheeks, see picture for position.

Antennae (make 2)

The antennae are crocheted in rows, not in rounds.

Row 1: using yarn A and a 2mm (UK 14, US 0) hook, ch 5, plus 1 ch to turn (6 sts).

Row 2: starting in the second chain from the hook, sl st in each st (5 sts).

Fasten off, leaving an end for sewing. Sew the antennae on the head between rounds 6 and 7, 8 sts apart.

Shell

First part of the shell

The flower is a granny circle. See technique on page 16 on how to attach a new colour.
Round 1: using yarn B and a 2mm (UK 14, US 0) hook, ch 4, sl st into the first st to make a circle (4 sts).
Round 2: ch 3, work the following sts into the centre of the circle: 1 tr, ch 1, *2 tr, ch 1*, five times, make a sl st into top of beginning ch 3 to complete the circle. Fasten off (18 sts).
Round 3: attach yarn C into the first chain space, ch 3, 1 tr, ch 1, 2 tr in that same chain space, crochet *2 tr, ch 1, 2 tr* in each chain space, sl st into top of beginning ch 3 (30 sts).
Round 4: attach yarn D into a chain space between two pairs of trebles (see picture), ch 3, 6 tr in the same chain space, crochet 7 tr (cluster) in each chain space, sl st into top of beginning ch 3 (42 sts).
Round 5: attach yarn E into the first st of a cluster, ch 1, 1 dc in the same st, 6 dc (1 dc in each tr of the first cluster of the previous round), make 1 deep dc (put the hook in the chain space of round 3, see picture), continue the round like this (1 dc in each tr of the previous round, 1 deep dc), sl st into top of beginning ch 3 (48 sts).

From this point on, you'll work in spirals and with v-shaped dc. It is important to use v-shaped dc stitches from here on, because it accentuates the contours of the flower.

Round 6: change to yarn F, 1 dc in each st (48 sts).
Round 7: *7 dc, 2 dc in next st*, six times (54 sts).
Rounds 8–10: 1 dc in each st (54 sts).
Fasten off, weave in the ends.

Second part of the shell

Crochet the first half of the shell again, but this time fasten off and leave a long tail for sewing the two parts together. See technique on page 12 on how to sew open pieces together.

Sew the shell onto the body from rounds 19–35. Then glue the shell to the body so that it doesn't wobble sideways.

Sun hat

Round 1: using yarn E and a 2mm (UK 14, US 0) hook, 6 dc in an adjustable ring (6 sts).
Round 2: 2 dc in each st (12 sts).
Round 3: 1 dc in each st (12 sts).
Round 4: change to yarn F, 1 dc in each st (12 sts).
Round 5: change to yarn E, 1 dc in the front loop of each stitch (12 sts).
Round 6: 2 dc in each st (24 sts).
Round 7: sl st in each st (24 sts).
Fasten off with an invisible finish, weave in the end. Stuff the sun hat gently and glue it on the head between the antennae and the shell, over rounds 6–14 (see picture for position).

Shane Sharky

Shane is a very shy and sensitive little shark. She always swims with her noise-cancelling headphones on, enjoying the silence, but looking very cool at the same time. Her favourite moment of the day is going home to her fuzzy blanket and watching some episodes of *Grey's Anatomy*.

You will need

– Basic kit (see page 8)

– 2mm (UK 14, US 0) crochet hook

– 2.5mm (UK 12/13, US 1/2) crochet hook

– Yarn:

• 2 balls of 5-ply (sport), 78% cotton, 22% acrylic, 50g/1¾oz/130m/142yd. I used Scheepjes Stone Washed in smokey quartz 802 (A) and moon stone 801 (B)

• 1 ball of 4-ply (fingering), 100% mercerized cotton, 50g/1¾oz/125m/137yd. I used Scheepjes Catona in old rose 408 (C)

• 2 balls of 4-ply (fingering), 100% cotton, 50g/1¾oz/170m/186yd. I used Scheepjes Organicon in amaranth 245 (D) and golden sun 237 (E)

– 2 safety eyes, 8mm (5⁄16in)

– Black embroidery thread

I am 21cm (8in) tall

Body

Shane is crocheted in v-shaped double crochet, because it looks better when using the short row technique (see page 16).

Round 1: using yarn A and a 2.5mm (UK 12/13, US 1/2) hook, 6 dc in an adjustable ring (6 sts).

Round 2: *1 dc, 2 dc in next st*, three times (9 sts).

Round 3: *2 dc, 2 dc in next st*, three times (12 sts).

Round 4: *3 dc, 2 dc in next st*, three times (15 sts).

Round 5: *4 dc, 2 dc in next st*, three times (18 sts).

Round 6: in this round, we'll start with the short row technique, 9 dc, turn, *no* turning chain.

A: On the wrong side of the work: from this point on we work in rows: starting in the first st from the hook, 8 dc, leave the last st of this row unworked, turn, *no* turning ch.

B: 8 dc (1 dc in every st of the row above), 9 dc (18 sts).

Round 7: 1 dc in each st (18 sts).

Round 8: *5 dc, 2 dc in next st*, three times (21 sts).

Round 9: 11 dc, turn, *no* turning ch.

A: On the wrong side of the work: starting in the first st, 10 dc, leave the last st of this row unworked, turn, *no* turning ch.

B: 10 dc (1 dc in every st of the row above), 10 dc (21 sts).

Round 10: *6 dc, 2 dc in next st*, three times (24 sts).

Round 11: 1 dc in each st (24 sts).

Round 12: *3 dc, 2 dc in next st*, six times (30 sts).

Round 13: 15 dc, turn, *no* turning ch.

A: On the wrong side of the work: starting in the first st, 14 dc, leave the last st of this row unworked, turn, *no* turning ch.

B: 14 dc (1 dc in every st of the row above), 15 dc (30 sts).

Round 14: *4 dc, 2 dc in next st*, six times (36 sts).

Rounds 15 and 16: 1 dc in each st (36 sts).

Round 17: 18 dc, turn, *no* turning ch.

A: On the wrong side of the work: starting in the first st, 17 dc, leave the last st of this row unworked, turn, *no* turning ch.

B: 17 dc (each in every st of the row above), 18 dc (36 sts).

Round 18: *5 dc, 2 dc in next st*, six times (42 sts).

Round 19: 1 dc in each st (42 sts).

Round 20: *6 dc, 2 dc in next st*, six times (48 sts).

Rounds 21 and 22: 1 dc in each st (48 sts).

Round 23: 14 dc, dc2tog, 5 dc, dc2tog, *6 dc, dc2tog*, twice, 9 dc (44 sts).

Round 24: 13 dc, dc2tog, 20 dc, dc2tog, 7 dc (42 sts).

Round 25: 1 dc in each st (42 sts).

Round 26: *5 dc, dc2tog*, six times (36 sts).

Round 27: *4 dc, dc2tog*, six times (30 sts).

Fasten off. Stuff the tail and body firmly.

Head

Round 1: using yarn A and a 2.5mm (UK 12/13, US 1/2) hook, 6 dc in an adjustable ring (6 sts).
Round 2: 2 dc in each st (12 sts).
Round 3: *1 dc, 2 dc in next st*, six times (18 sts).
Round 4: *2 dc, 2 dc in next st*, six times (24 sts).
Round 5: *3 dc, 2 dc in next st*, six times (30 sts).
Round 6: *4 dc, 2 dc in next st*, six times (36 sts).
Round 7: *5 dc, 2 dc in next st*, six times (42 sts).
Round 8: *6 dc, 2 dc in next st*, six times (48 sts).
Rounds 9–15: 1 dc in each st (48 sts).
Rounds 16–19: change to yarn B, 1 dc in each st (48 sts).
Round 20: *6 dc, dc2tog*, six times (42 sts).
Round 21: 1 dc in each st (42 sts).
Round 22: *5 dc, dc2tog*, six times (36 sts).
Round 23: *4 dc, dc2tog*, six times (30 sts).
Fasten off, leaving an end for sewing.
Attach the safety eyes between rounds 14 and 15 with 8 sts in between.
Stuff the head firmly. Once you have attached the cheeks and headphones, sew the head onto the body.

Cheeks (make 2)

Round 1: using yarn C and a 2.5mm (UK 12/13, US 1/2) hook, 8 dc in an adjustable ring (8 sts).
Fasten off with an invisible finish, weave in the ends.
Glue the cheeks onto the face, diagonally below the eyes (see picture for position).
With black thread, embroider the mouth in the centre between rounds 16 and 17, 2 sts wide.

Headphone ear pads (make 2)

Round 1: using yarn D and a 2mm (UK 14, US 0) hook, 6 dc in an adjustable ring (6 sts).
Round 2: 2 dc in each st (12 sts).
Round 3: *1 dc, 2 dc in next st*, six times (18 sts).
Round 4: *2 dc, 2 dc in next st*, six times (24 sts).
Round 5: change to yarn E, 1 dc in bl of each st (24 sts).
Rounds 6 and 7: 1 dc in each st (24 sts).
Fasten off with an invisible finish, weave in the ends.

Headphone headband

The headband is crocheted in rows.
Row 1: using yarn D and a 2mm (UK 14, US 0) hook, ch 3, plus ch 1 to turn (3 sts).
Row 2: starting in the second ch from the hook, 3 dc, ch 1 to turn (3 sts).
Repeat row 2 until the headband fits. I crocheted 40 rows.
Fasten off, weave in the ends. Glue the headband on the head, leaning slightly forwards. See picture for position.
Sew the ear pads over the ends onto the head, over rounds 12–19.

Tail fins (make 2)

Round 1: using yarn A and a 2.5mm (UK 12/13, US 1/2) hook, 4 dc in an adjustable ring (4 sts).
Round 2: *1 dc, 2 dc in next st*, twice (6 sts).
Round 3: *1 dc, 2 dc in next st*, three times (9 sts).
Round 4: *1 dc, 2 dc in next st* two times, 5 dc (11 sts).
Round 5: 1 dc in each st (11 sts).
Round 6: 6 dc, dc2tog, 3 dc (10 sts).
Round 7: 1 dc in each st (10 sts).
Fasten off, leaving an end for sewing.
Do not stuff. Flatten and sew onto either side of the body over rounds 1–5.

Upper fin

Round 1: using yarn A and a 2.5mm (UK 12/13, US 1/2) hook, 4 dc in an adjustable ring (4 sts).
Round 2: *1 dc, 2 dc in next st*, twice (6 sts).
Round 3: *1 dc, 2 dc in next st*, three times (9 sts).
Round 4: *2 dc, 2 dc in next st*, three times (12 sts).
Round 5: 1 dc in each st (12 sts).
Round 6: *3 dc, 2 dc in next st*, three times (15 sts).
Round 7: 5 dc, 5 htr, 5 dc (15 sts).
Fasten off, leaving an end for sewing.
Do not stuff. Flatten and sew vertically onto the back of the body over rounds 17–25 from bottom to top, see picture for position.

Pectoral side fins (make 2)

Round 1: using yarn A and a 2.5mm (UK 12/13, US 1/2) hook, 4 dc in an adjustable ring (4 sts).
Round 2: *1 dc, 2 dc in next st*, twice (6 sts).
Round 3: *1 dc, 2 dc in next st*, three times (9 sts).
Round 4: 8 dc, 2 dc in next st (10 sts).
Round 5: 1 dc in each st (10 sts).
Round 6: *4 dc, 2 dc in next st*, twice (12 sts).
Rounds 7 and 8: 1 dc in each st (12 sts).
Do not stuff. Flatten and sew vertically onto either side of the body over rounds 20–25 from bottom to top, see picture for position.

Belly

The belly is crocheted in rows.
Row 1: using yarn B and a 2.5mm (UK 12/13, US 1/2) hook, ch 10, plus ch 1 to turn (10 sts).
Rows 2–5: starting in the second ch from the hook, 10 dc, ch 1 to turn (10 sts).
Row 6: 2 dc, dc2tog, 2 dc, dc2tog, 2 dc, ch 1 to turn (8 sts).
Rows 7–9: 1 dc in each st, ch 1 to turn (8 sts).
Row 10: 1 dc, dc2tog, 2 dc, dc2tog, 1 dc, 1 ch to turn (6 sts).
Rows 11 and 12: 1 dc in each st, 1 ch to turn (6 sts).
Row 13: 1 dc, dc2tog, dc2tog, 1 dc (4 sts).
At the end of row 13, work in dc around the belly, work 2 dc in the corners to smooth the curve.
Sew the belly onto the body, over rounds 3–16, see picture for position.

Theodore Teddy

Theo is a world-famous stuntbear and is not afraid of ANYthing. He jumps out of helicopters, swims with alligators and climbs mountains. He has one little secret though: he doesn't like the dark. Therefore, he always wears a glow-in-the-dark-friendship bracelet. He carries a bag full of yarn so he can weave a bracelet for anyone else who isn't keen on the dark.

You will need

– Basic kit (see page 8)

– 2.5mm (UK 12/13, US 1/2) crochet hook

– Yarn:

• 2 balls of 5-ply (sport), 100% cotton, 50g/1¾oz/130m/142yd. I used Scheepjes Stone Washed in brown agate 822 (A) and blue apatite 805 (B)

• 3 small balls of 4-ply (fingering), 100% mercerized cotton, 25g/⅞oz/62.5m/68yd. I used Scheepjes Catona in old rose 408 (C), deep ocean green 391 (D) and petrol blue 400 (E)

• 1 ball of 4-ply (fingering), 100% polyester, 50g/1¾oz/105m/115yd. I used Scheepjes Glow Up in luminescent white 1001 (F)

– 2 safety eyes, 7mm (¼in)

– Black embroidery thread

– Brown felt

I am 20cm (8in) tall

Legs and lower body

Start with the first leg.
Round 1: using yarn A and a 2.5mm (UK 12/13, US 1/2) hook, 8 dc in an adjustable ring (8 sts).
Close the ring with a sl st, ch 1.
Round 2: 1 dc in the back loop of each st (8 sts).
Round 3: *3 dc, 2 dc in next st*, twice (10 sts).
Round 4: *4 dc, 2 dc in next st*, twice (12 sts).
Round 5: *5 dc, 2 dc in next st*, twice (14 sts).
Round 6: 1 dc in each st (14 sts).
Fasten off. Crochet the second leg, but do not fasten off.
Round 7: join the two legs as follows: ch 4 at the end of the second leg, 14 dc (one in every stitch of the leg), ch 4, 14 dc in the second leg (4 + 14 + 4 + 14 = 36 sts). See page 15 for technique.
Round 8: 1 dc in each st (36 sts).
Round 9: *8 dc, 2 dc in next st*, three times, 9 dc (39 sts).
Round 10: 10 dc, 2 dc in next st, 9 dc, 2 dc in next st, 8 dc, 2 dc in next st, 9 dc (42 sts).
Round 11: 11 dc, 2 dc in next st, *9 dc, 2 dc in next st*, twice, 10 dc (45 sts).
Round 12: 11 dc, 2 dc in next st, *10 dc, 2 dc in next st*, twice, 11 dc (48 sts).
Rounds 13–23: 1 dc in each st (48 sts).
Round 24: 14 dc, dc2tog, 5 dc, dc2tog, *6 dc, dc2tog*, twice, 9 dc (44 sts).
Round 25: 1 dc in each st (44 sts).
Stitch up the hole between the two legs and start stuffing the legs and lower body.
Round 26: 13 dc, dc2tog, 20 dc, dc2tog, 7 dc (42 sts).
Round 27: 1 dc in each st (42 sts).
Round 28: *5 dc, dc2tog*, six times (36 sts).
Round 29: *4 dc, dc2tog*, six times (30 sts).
Round 30: 1 dc in each st (30 sts).
Fasten off.
Stuff the legs and body firmly.

Head

Round 1: using yarn A and a 2.5mm (UK 12/13, US 1/2) hook, 6 dc in an adjustable ring (6 sts).
Round 2: 2 dc in each st (12 sts).
Round 3: *1 dc, 2 dc in next st*, six times (18 sts).
Round 4: *2 dc, 2 dc in next st*, six times (24 sts).
Round 5: *3 dc, 2 dc in next st*, six times (30 sts).
Round 6: *4 dc, 2 dc in next st*, six times (36 sts).
Round 7: *5 dc, 2 dc in next st*, six times (42 sts).
Round 8: *6 dc, 2 dc in next st*, six times (48 sts).
Rounds 9–18: 1 dc in each st (48 sts).
Round 19: *6 dc, dc2tog*, six times (42 sts).
Round 20: 1 dc in each st (42 sts).
Round 21: *5 dc, dc2tog*, six times (36 sts).
Rounds 22 and 23: 1 dc in each st (36 sts).
Round 24: *4 dc, dc2tog*, six times (30 sts).
Fasten off, leaving an end for sewing. Stuff the head firmly.
Attach the safety eyes between rounds 15 and 16 with 10 sts in between. Using the brown felt and the template below, cut out the snout. Embroider the snout and mouth. Glue the felt centrally between the eyes, over rounds 16–20. Sew the head onto the body (after you have attached the cheeks and ears).

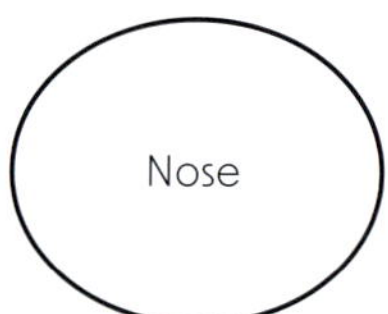

Cheeks (make 2)

Round 1: using yarn C and a 2.5mm (UK 12/13, US 1/2) hook, 8 dc in an adjustable ring (8 sts).
Fasten off with an invisible finish, weave in the ends.
Glue the cheeks onto the face, diagonally below the eyes (see picture for position).

Ears (make 2)

Round 1: using yarn A and a 2.5mm (UK 12/13, US 1/2) hook, 6 dc in an adjustable ring (6 sts).
Round 2: 2 dc in each st (12 sts).
Round 3: 1 dc in each st (12 sts).
Fasten off, leaving an end for sewing.
Sew the ears onto the head on either side across rounds 7 and 8 with 10 sts in between.

Arms (make 2)

Round 1: using yarn A and a 2.5mm (UK 12/13, US 1/2) hook, 5 dc in an adjustable ring (5 sts).
Round 2: 2 dc in each st (10 sts).
Rounds 3–13: 1 dc in each st (10 sts).
Fasten off, leaving an end for sewing.
Gently stuff the front of the arms.
Sew the arms onto the body on either side at round 30.

Tail

Round 1: using yarn A and a 2.5mm (UK 12/13, US 1/2) hook, 6 dc in an adjustable ring (6 sts).
Rounds 2–11: 1 dc in each st (6 sts).
Fasten off, leaving an end for sewing.
Sew the tail onto the body over rounds 11–14.

Glow in the dark friendship bracelet

Step 1: cut three 15cm (6in) strands of yarn (I've used yarn B, E and F).
Step 2: tie the strands together and braid them until the bracelet fits around Theodore's arm. Make a knot. Tie the bracelet around the paw, but let some loose ends hang out.

Bag

Round 1: using yarn D and a 2.5mm (UK 12/13, US 1/2) hook, 6 dc in an adjustable ring (6 sts).
Round 2: 2 dc in each st (12 sts).
Round 3: *1 dc, 2 dc in next st*, six times (18 sts).
Round 4: *2 dc, 2 dc in next st*, six times (24 sts).
Rounds 5–10: 1 dc in each st (24 sts).
Round 11: 3 dc, ch 40, skip next 6 sts, 6 dc, ch 40, skip next 6 sts, 3 dc.
Fasten off with an invisible finish. Weave in the ends.
Make small balls of yarn with yarns B, E and F. Place or glue them into the bag.